# OFF THE BEATEN PATH®
# METRO NEW YORK →

# Help Us Keep This Guide Up to Date

We would love to hear from you concerning your experiences with this guide and how you feel it could be improved and kept up to date. Please send your comments and suggestions to:

editorial@GlobePequot.com

Thanks for your input, and happy travels!

FIRST EDITION

# OFF THE BEATEN PATH®
# METRO NEW YORK ➡

## A GUIDE TO UNIQUE PLACES

## SUSAN FINCH

gpp®
travel

Guilford, Connecticut

All the information in this guidebook is subject to change. We recommend that you call ahead to obtain current information before traveling.

To buy books in quantity for corporate use
or incentives, call **(800) 962-0973**
or e-mail **premiums@GlobePequot.com**.

Editor: Kevin Sirois
Project Editor: Lynn Zelem
Layout: Joanna Beyer
Text design: Linda R. Loiewski
Maps: Equator Graphics © Morris Book Publishing, LLC

Library of Congress Cataloging-in-Publication Data is available on file.
ISBN 978-0-7627-5876-0

Printed in the United States of America
10 9 8 7 6 5 4 3 2 1

# About the Author

Susan Finch is a freelance travel and lifestyle writer living in Brooklyn, New York, with an affinity for offbeat attractions. She's the author of *Off the Beaten Path Upstate New York*, *Best Easy Day Hikes: Long Island*, and *Best Easy Day Hikes: Columbus*.

# Acknowledgments

I want to extend my endless appreciation to my husband and travel partner, Drew Padrutt. Without your support, friendship, patience, and stubbornness, I would have never known just how much there is to love about New York City. I wouldn't want to explore it with anyone else. Thanks to Katie Mantell and all my friends who contributed their expert insight and enthusiasm to this guide, I couldn't have done this without you. I'd also like to thank everyone at Family TravelForum.com for believing in me and giving me a start with something I hold dear, travel writing. And a big thanks to Globe Pequot Press, New York State Tourism, The New York State Office of Parks, Recreation, and Historic Preservation, and all the men and women who keep this city up and running.

# Contents

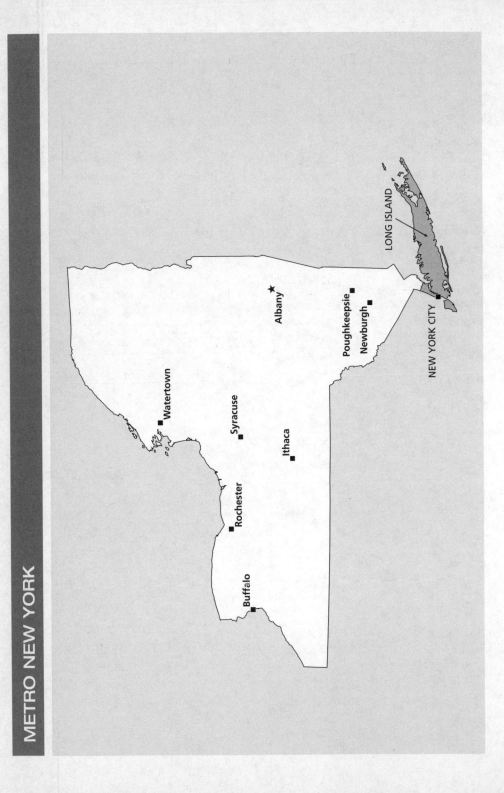

METRO NEW YORK

LONG ISLAND

NEW YORK CITY

Poughkeepsie
Newburgh

Albany

Watertown

Syracuse

Ithaca

Rochester

Buffalo

# Introduction

New York City's standing as one of the largest cities in the world makes it "on the beaten path" by definition alone. You will be hard pressed to find a hidden neighborhood, secret gem, or unknown attraction that no one has ever heard about. But you will uncover quirky locations, unusual attractions, fiercely protected insider secrets, and plenty of tangled history to unravel. Fortunately for tourists looking for something a little different, this city hides its hidden gems in plain sight.

Tourists tend to take the beaten path because of a lack of time and resources to branch out and truly explore. While seeing the Empire State Building, Statue of Liberty, and Museum of Modern Art are worthwhile ventures, the city has a long and intricate history full of nearly forgotten islands, tucked away beaches, wildlife sanctuaries, a working farm, subway tunnel tours, crumbling ruins, and bizarre haunts in the middle of one of the most visited cities on the planet. And you don't have to venture very far off the beaten path. You can even find unusual stops right in Times Square.

Be warned there are more New York City attractions, neighborhoods, and events to take in than time will ever permit. Do not labor under any delusion that you can see everything the city has to offer in one trip, let alone twenty. Locals often bemoan (with a smirk) that having a social life and exploring the city is like holding down a second full-time job. A night at home usually brings on acute anxiety of what the city is doing without them.

But that anxiety of wondering what the city is doing without you is also part of New York City's perpetual beauty and charm. You will never run out of attractions, neighborhoods, theater, music, restaurants, pubs, and parks to explore. You can revisit this beloved city I call home time and time again with new eyes and forget it's not your very first time. As you travel her paths and attractions, the city will envelop you in her arms and reveal bits of hidden architecture, little known attractions, and unexpected finds.

For first timers, tackle the city by making a list of your interests from art, history, restaurants, or top attractions. Mix favorite tourist haunts with a list of attractions most visitors would never find. This includes stretching your horizons into the outer-boroughs to Brooklyn, Queens, the Bronx, and Staten Island. Coming to New York and only visiting Manhattan is denying the rich diversity and flavor the city offers. Don't mistake their position over the River or just beyond Manhattan as second-rate locales. Some of the best of what the city offers lies in its outer-boroughs. And take a moment to consider that most tourists who dislike the intensity of New York City never venture past attractions found on top 10 lists that squeeze in crowds by the thousands.

There is much to see and do in isolated and tranquil spots scattered across the city.

For visitors who have already explored New York City a handful of times and are ready to hedge toward its lesser known attractions, use this book as a resource to point you in new directions and paths you've yet to traverse. Find the completely bizarre points of interests (like a forbidden cemetery on a desolate island of the Bronx) and learn something new about more familiar attractions you may have never known. Like the cold war era ration that was found in the Brooklyn Bridge in 2006, or the piece of the Berlin Wall in Battery Park. Or how about the African Burial Ground in the Financial District? Pepper path-worn favorite attractions with unique twists you never knew about. Until now.

# MANHATTAN →

Start your journey through the city downtown in Lower Manhattan, where it all started. In 1609, the Dutch launched their first expedition to New York by the East India Company pioneered by Henry Hudson and called the area New Amsterdam and began building a fort in Battery Park, developing their commerce with Native Americans, and building the first church and homes. At the *South Street Seaport* (Fulton and South Streets, Pier 17; 212-SEA-PORT; www.southstreetseaport.com), you can learn more about the foundations of the district and settlement of the prominent Schermerhorn family (which is also a street name and subway stop in Brooklyn). The Schermerhorns were shipmasters and chandlers who purchased most of today's Seaport District and, in 1810, developed a block of conjoined buildings called Schermerhorn Row. Over the years, the seaport fell into disrepair and neglect before undergoing renovations. In 1967 the *South Street Seaport Museum* (12 Fulton St.; 212-748-8786; www.southstreetseaportmuseum.org) was founded to save the historic buildings in the area. Visit the South Street Seaport Museum to learn more about the district's history and founding members.

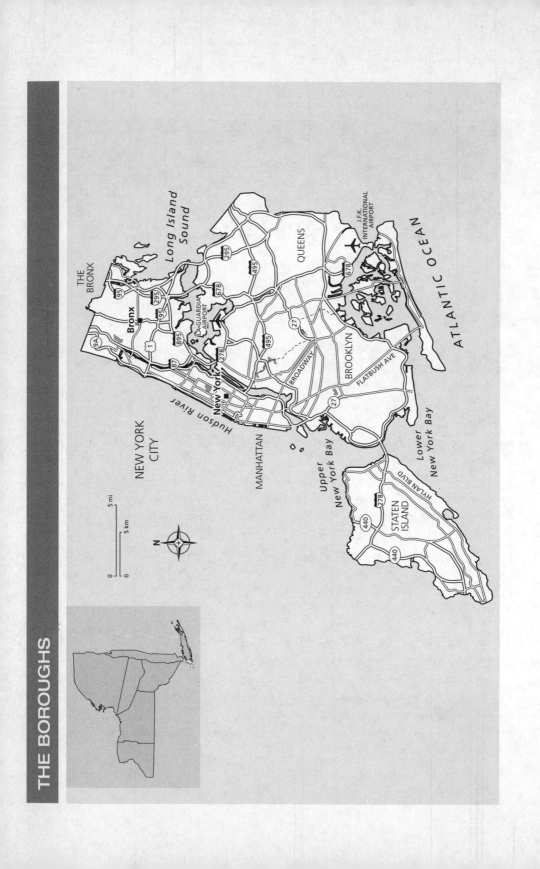

At the entrance to the seaport district near the museum, look for the nearly forgotten *Titanic Memorial Lighthouse* (www.southstreetseaportmuseum .org/index1.aspx?BD=9176), forever memorializing its passengers, officers, and crews. The catastrophe shook New York to its core, funds were raised, and the lighthouse was erected in 1913 on the roof of the Seamen's Church Institute along the East River. Between the years 1913 and 1967, a time ball at the top of the lighthouse dropped to signal twelve o'clock to the ships passing by. The memorial was eventually donated to the museum and moved to its current location.

From January to March, the South Street Seaport Museum is open Friday through Sunday from 10 a.m. to 5 p.m. with all galleries open. On Mondays from 10 a.m. to 5 p.m., only the Schermerhorn Row Galleries are open. From April to December, the museum is closed on Monday and is open Tuesday to Sunday from 10 a.m. to 6 p.m. Tickets are $12 adults, $10 seniors and students, $8 children ages 5 to 12. See the ships for $8. To get to the South Street Seaport Museum by subway, take the 2, 3, 4, 5, J, Z, or M trains to Fulton Street or A and C trains to Broadway-Nassau.

But what about the earliest locals? Long before the Dutch ever set foot on the island and the Schermerhorns set up shop in the Seaport, the Lenape people lived in Manhattan. To honor their heritage, one of the first-rank museums in the city, but perhaps the least known is the Smithsonian Institution's National Museum of the American Indian, George Gustav Heye Center. George Heye was an heir to an oil fortune who worked as a railroad construction engineer in the Southwest. In 1897 he bought the first of his artifacts, a contemporary Navajo buckskin shirt, and from that point he went on to develop a collection that encompassed all things native, from Alaska to Tierra del Fuego. He bought items that had just been made and from archaeological finds dating from long before the European discovery of America. Heye founded his museum in 1916, and it opened to the public six years later. At that stage, the collector had owned some 400,000 objects; today the museum has more than a million individual items.

## AUTHORS' FAVORITES NEW YORK CITY

| | |
|---|---|
| Jamaica Bay Wildlife Refuge Center | Bohemian Hall and Beer Garden, Astoria |
| Atlantic Avenue Tunnel Tour | |
| Lower East Side Tenement Museum | Governors Island |

## The Big Apple

The city's nickname was first coined in the 1920s, when John Fitzgerald, a sports-writer for the *Morning Telegraph,* overheard stable-hands in New Orleans refer to New York City's racetracks as "the Big Apple." He named his column "Around the Big Apple." A decade later, jazz musicians who used the slang word *apple* for any city they were touring, adopted the term to refer to New York City, and especially Harlem, as the jazz capital of the world. The saying goes, "There are many apples on the tree of success, but when you pick New York City, you pick the Big Apple."

*The National Museum of the American Indian,* George Gustav Heye Center, at the Alexander Hamilton U.S. Custom House, One Bowling Green (212-514-3700; www.nmai.si.edu), is open daily except Christmas from 10 a.m. to 5 p.m., and Thursday until 8 p.m. Admission is free. By train, take the 4 and 5 trains to Bowling Green, the 1 to South Ferry, the R and W to Whitehall Street, or the J, M, Z to Broad Street.

More than 2,000 photographs, an expansive collection of artifacts, original documentary films, and individual narratives are utilized to create a picture of Jewish life and culture from the late 1880s to the present at the Museum of Jewish Heritage, A Living Memorial to the Holocaust. The museum is in Battery Park City overlooking the Statue of Liberty and Ellis Island. *The Museum of Jewish Heritage, A Living Memorial to the Holocaust,* 36 Battery Place (646-437-4200; www.mjhnyc.org), is open Sunday through Tuesday and Thursday 10 a.m. to 5:45 p.m., Wednesday 10 a.m. to 8 p.m., and Friday and the eve of Jewish holidays 10 a.m. to 3 p.m. Admission is $12 for adults, $10 for seniors, $7 for students, and free for children 12 and under. Admission is free on Wednesday from 4 to 8 p.m. By subway, take the 4, 5 to Bowling Green, the R, W to Whitehall Street, the 1 to South Ferry, or the J, M, Z to Broad Street.

Battery Park is also home to museums with a modern edge reflecting the city's vertical history, including the *Skyscraper Museum.* This architectural homage features iconic pictures of construction workers sharing lunch while their feet dangle off tall beams, historic information on how the city was built, and timetables. You can also learn how skyscrapers are measured by the Council on Tall Buildings and Urban Habitat. Photos of the city's original skyscrapers, the World Trade Center, and info on New York's urban jungle are also on display. It won't be lost on visitors that the cozy museum houses an in-depth look at some of the tallest buildings in the world.

The museum was initially in temporary spaces from 1997 to 2003 before settling in Battery Park in 2004. The Skyscraper Museum (212-968-1961; www

.skyscraper.org) is located at 39 Battery Place inside the Ritz Carlton. The museum is open from noon to 6 p.m. from Wednesday to Sunday. Admission runs $5 for adults and $2.50 for students and seniors. Take the 4 or 5 trains to Bowling Green, the 1, R or W to Rector Street.

Stroll over to Battery Park and after a trip to the Statue of Liberty and Ellis Island, head to the *Irish Hunger Memorial* (corner of 290 Vesey St. and North End Avenue; 212-417-2000; www.batteryparkcity.org/page/page4_6.html). Walk west to the hem of green hugging the city, a 32-acre park stretching north. Locals, families, and tourists gather for a day strolling the grounds, playing Frisbee, and enjoying twenty works of public art. One of the installations, the Irish Hunger Memorial garden, created by Brian Tolle, honors those who died during

## reachforthesky

In the mid-1800s, Lucas Glockner, a German-born tailor, bought a lot at 97 Orchard St. on the Lower East Side that measured 25 by 100 feet. The lot was originally intended for single-family town houses, but Glockner erected a six-story tenement with apartments for twenty-two families, as well as two storefronts in the basement. Each floor featured four three-room apartments with a total of 325 square feet each. Only one of the three rooms had windows.

An Gorta Mór (or The Great Hunger) and brings attention to those who are hungry in the world today. It's noted that many Irish immigrated to the Untied States to escape their deplorable conditions and find work to feed their families.

The memorial aptly sits on half an acre of land, a nod to the Irish Poor Law mandated by Sir William Gregory stating that anyone with more than a half acre of land could not receive aid or assistance. Visit the roofless stone cottage from County Mayo in Ireland and, if you're of Irish descent, take note of the stones from Ireland's thirty-two counties. Read miles of posted poems about famine, read quotes, and listen to the audio track recounting stories of

## Among the Earliest Arrivals

The country's oldest Jewish congregation, *Congregation Shearith Israel* ("Remnant of Israel"), dates to September 12, 1654, when a group of newly arrived Jews from Spain and Portugal held a New Year service in New Amsterdam. The oldest gravestone in the congregation's first cemetery, at 55–57 St. James Place, bears the date 1683. The remains of many colonial-era Jews interred here had to be moved to newer cemeteries in Manhattan to make room for road construction.

our world's hunger. This unique piece of outdoor art and tranquil garden is an oasis in the bustling Financial District.

At 36 Battery Park, The Museum of Jewish Heritage features a **Garden of Stones.** This permanent outdoor exhibit features boulders throughout its garden. Upon first glance, the boulders may look like nothing more than carefully placed ornaments for a lovely tree-lined garden. But each boulder is hollow and holds a Dwarf Oak sapling that increasingly grows through a hole located at the top of each rock. The tree will eventually fuse to the stone and symbolize how nature survives during impossible situations. The trees were planted by the commissioned Garden of Stones artist, Andy Goldsworthy and Holocaust survivors and their families. Over the years, come back to the garden to see how the saplings have grown and flourished in the contemplative garden. For more information, call (212) 417-2000 or visit www.mjhnyc.org/garden/index.html.

Also nearby, look for the park's **Stuart Crawford Police Memorial** complete with a running fountain and linear flume. Built in 1977, the water symbolizes a rookie police officer becoming a seasoned officer. The shallow pool represents the officer's death, and two granite walls hold the names and dates of slain officers.

Did you see that large piece of painted wall during your stroll through the Esplanade? That unexpected chunk of history nestled in Battery Park is part of Germany's **Berlin Wall.** A 12-foot-high, 8-foot-wide, and nearly 3-ton piece of the wall was given as a gift to Battery Park City by the German Consulate to honor the 15th anniversary of the fallen Wall. This specific piece of the Wall once kept East Germans from fleeing between Potsdamer Platz and Leipziger Platz.

As you continue your journey through Battery Park, note how the expanse of Hudson River Park reaches from Battery Park all the way to about 59th Street. A large pedestrian walkway and bike lane allows for Hudson River views on one side, and Manhattan on the other. I really love walking from Battery Park to the Chelsea area of the park during the summer. When not undergoing construction, trapeze schools, vendors, batting cages, and bike rentals set up shop. There's also seasonal free kayaking at the **New York Downtown Boat House** (www.downtownboathouse.org) at Pier 40, Pier 96, and 72nd Street. The boathouse also has lockers, though you'll need to bring your own lock. You can go on a single or tandem kayak ride for thirty minutes, free.

I had never been kayaking in my life until testing the waters on the Hudson, but the volunteers made it easy for me to learn and feel comfortable in just minutes. Follow the rules and stay in the pre-designated area tucked away

## Giving Back to the Arts

Many of the museums in New York are free during certain days of the week or month; check their Web sites in advance. But if you can't coordinate your trip to a free museum day, take note that many advertise a Suggested or Recommended Donation of a specified amount. This is simply a suggestion, and you are allowed to pay whatever you wish. Just say, "I would like to make a $5 donation," or whatever amount of your choosing. But keep in mind that generously supporting the city museums means supporting its arts and giving back on your vacation.

from the onslaught of summer boaters (surely irritating to experienced and seasoned kayakers) and if you manage to fall in, a rescue effort will ensue.

If you're planning to visit the Brooklyn Bridge from the footbridge on the Manhattan side, take a moment to step into *City Hall Park* (31 Chambers St.; www.nycgovparks.org/parks/cityhallpark/) first. The surrounding government buildings date back to 1812 and hug a landscape of green grass, colorful flowers, and park benches. From 1653 to 1699, the park served as a pasture for livestock, referred to as The Commons. A Native American trail over on the western edge is now present-day Broadway. Over the recent decades, new finds and hidden secrets were unearthed. In 1989, an almshouse structure, shelter for the poor, was uncovered. Eventually the grounds became a debtor's prison, which later became the House of Records. Retrace history to the soldier's barracks, as well as the protest site for the Stamp Act in 1765. New Yorkers erected the first "Liberty Pole" to celebrate their independence and included a vane with the word "liberty" inscribed on it. Today, you can look over toward City Hall and Broadway for its replica built in 1921. Revolutionary prisoners were also held in the gallows on these grounds. By 1803, City Hall began its first stages of development, paving the way for New Yorkers to gather and discuss politics and hold public meetings; it was also the start point for New York's funeral procession of President Lincoln. In 1961, City Hall was designated a city and national landmark. Today you can sit down with a coffee for a fascinating session in people watching. Aside from the usual staples of government workers and jurors, you can see newlyweds, freshly eloped, pour into the park with fresh smiles plastered across their faces.

New York is never lacking in historical finds, even newly discovered ones. A piece of Manhattan's nearly forgotten history was recently uncovered after the startling discovery of an African Burial Ground, prompting the area to secure a spot as a national historic site. In 1991, archaeologists uncovered the largest known intact colonial African cemetery in America, right in New York

City. It was first discovered during construction on a federal office building at 290 Broadway in the Financial District. Workers uncovered bones that led to over 400 hundred remains of men, women, and children in a 6.6-acre burial ground. Investigators determined the remains were those of free and enslaved Africans dating to the 17th and 18th centuries.

The African Burial Ground is now celebrated as one of the most signifi-cant finds in American history. Among the collection is Burial #335, holding a woman 25 to 35 years old with the remains of an infant in the crook of her right arm. Archaeologists assume they were mother and child, and that both perhaps died during childbirth. The discovery also led to clues about the life of an enslaved woman—the woman's bones showed scarring at the muscle attach-ments and contained evidence of arthritis and nutritional stress, shedding light on the hard labor enslaved women performed in an 18th-century household. The burial grounds stretch approximately five city blocks from Broadway to Lafayette Street to the east, and from Chambers past Duane Street to the north.

*The African Burial Ground* (212-637-2019; www.africanburialground .gov) is located at 290 Broadway near the corner of Duane and Elk Streets in Lower Manhattan and is open to the public, free of charge, Monday to Friday from 9 a.m. until 4 p.m. The grounds are closed on Thanksgiving, Christmas, and New Year's Day. By public transportation, take the 4, 5, 6, R, and W train to Brooklyn Bridge/City Hall, the J, M, Z, or 1 train to Chambers Street, the 2, 3 train to Park Place, or the A, C, E to Chambers/World Trade Center.

At 1 Centre St. near the edge of the park and Broadway, look for the kiosk booth and ask the information clerk for directions, pick up maps, and inquire about a free tour with *Big Apple Greeters* (212-669-8159; www.big applegreeter.org). Over 300 volunteers offer insightful tours and work strictly

## Order in the Court

For a truly offbeat attraction that's sure to overexpose you to New York's grittier side of life, head to a session of *Night Court* (100 Centre St.; 646-386-4000; www .courts.state.ny.us/courts/1jd/index.shtml). Tourists have been frequenting the city's legal system for years, presumably to get a glimpse of the less savory side of the city. Legally, a person in New York can be held up to only forty-eight hours before being arraigned before a judge, and this means New York City courts are in action day and night. You'll find the courts full of legal aid lawyers, public defenders, and criminal lawyers with cases of drugs, robbery, and protest in tow. Night court hears the same cases as criminal court, just during the evening hours. It's not for the squeamish or faint at heart, as domestic violence, drug charges, and homicides are common. Night court is free to watch, and is in session from 5:30 p.m. to 1 a.m.

on a no-fee, no-tipping policy. The team of greeters speaks over twenty-two languages and tours are customized based on tourists' desired locations and interests when possible.

But there are a few rules to follow. Log onto their Web site and fill out a Visitor's Request Form and plan for a two- to four-hour tour between 9 a.m. and 3 p.m. The greeters do not accommodate visitors who are on a day trip or staying in the city less than two nights. Plan your free tour shortly after arriving in New York and let your local expert help acclimate you to the city. And if you don't know what neighborhood you want to see and where to go, you can let the Greeter pick for you instead.

The events on 9/11 changed New York City and our country forever, and it's important to remember not only those who died, but those who selflessly served.

For years, I couldn't quite bring myself to see the memorial at the World Trade Center, the anxieties from that day still fresh just below the surface. When I finally returned to the area to pay my respects, it was to the church directly across from the World Trade Center, **St. Paul's Chapel** (209 Broadway; 212-233-4164; www.saintpaulschapel.org). The Episcopal church housed the eight-month volunteer relief effort documented by the exhibit "Unwavering Spirit," with photos, memorabilia, and first-person accounts. Volunteers at the church worked around the clock to serve meals, pray with the firefighters and workers, and offer beds to our servicemen and -women.

The church is also New York's only remaining church from the Revolutionary era and Manhattan's oldest public building in continuous use and has a long history of political influence. George Washington worshipped at St. Paul's on his Inauguration Day on April 30, 1789, and continued to attend services when New York City was the country's capital. You can still see Washington's pew with a painting of the Great Seal of the United States, as well as the Governor's pew. Don't forget to take a stroll through the churchyard to see the final resting place of patriot soldiers.

**St. Paul's Chapel Ground Zero Ministry Exhibit** is free of charge and open from Monday to Saturday from 10 a.m. to 6 p.m., Sunday 7 a.m. to 6 p.m., and the churchyard closes daily at 5 p.m. Check their Web site to ensure the church is not unexpectedly closed for special events during your visit. Take the 2 or 3 trains to Park Place; or the 1, 9, 4, 5, or A to the Fulton Street-Broadway Nassau stop. You can also hop on the 6 to Brooklyn Bridge-City Hall subway station, the E to Chambers Street, or the R train to Cortlandt Street.

Experience a piece of New York's military history dating back to the 1600s. Once called Pagganck, or Nut Island, by Native Americans, **Governors Island** once held hickory, oak, and chestnut trees and was used for fishing camps by local tribes. In 1637, Holland native Wouter Van Twiller bought the island for his private use from the Native Americans of Manahatas for a handful of nails, two ax heads, and a string of beads. Eventually the Dutch government confiscated the island.

Due to its valuable strategic location, Governors Island changed hands to the British and walls were put up to fortify the grounds. During the Civil War, the island was used as a prison for captured Confederate soldiers, and during World War I and II, it was used as a military supply base. Military personnel were eventually relocated during the 1950s and the island was effectively closed. However, a working firehouse remained in operation from 2003 until about 2008, despite its desolate surroundings. Occasionally fires were staged in abandoned buildings to practice drills.

Governors Island (www.govisland.com) is open on Friday, Saturday, and Sunday from the end of May through early October (the island is also open to the public for free summer concerts and festivals during this time). The island is open from 10 a.m. to 5 p.m. on Friday and 10 a.m. to 7 p.m. on weekends. Check the Governors Island Web site for current ferry and event schedules. The Manhattan ferry leaves from the Battery Maritime Building at 10 South St. in lower Manhattan. Take the 1 train to South Ferry Station; the 4 or 5 train to Bowling Green Station; or the W or R train to Whitehall St. Station. The Brooklyn ferry leaves from Fulton Ferry Landing. You can catch the 2 or 3 to Clark Street in Brooklyn Heights, or the A or C to High Street to reach the landing. Bike rentals, snack bars, and free kayaking in designated areas are also available.

If Governors Island is closed during your visit, stop by the **Battery Maritime Building** to see a 140,000-square-foot Beaux-Arts landmark featuring cast iron columns, ceramic tiles, stucco, skylight, and plaster. During its completion in 1909, the building was used for ferries making the journey across the East River to 39th Street in Brooklyn until 1938. Aside from housing the seasonal Governors Island ferry, the building has acted as an exhibit space, including David Byrne's interactive installation, "Playing the Building." The historic building is set for a $110-million makeover complete with a rooftop restaurant and 140-room boutique hotel boasting water views and a prime downtown location. The architects plan to restore original detailing of the building while utilizing modern enhancements.

New York has always been creative about converting urban space into a green oasis. Running from Gransevoort Street in the Meatpacking District to 34th Street, **The Highline** (212-500-6035; www.thehighline.org) was originally constructed in the 1930s to lift freight trains off of Manhattan's streets. Property owners lobbied for its demolition in the 1980s. Eventually local residents

Joshua David and Robert Hammond founded Friends of the High Line and grew enough support to successfully preserve the area and secure a spot as a public park. A limited section opened to the public in the summer of 2009 with ongoing plans to open additional sections of the park over the years.

Visitors can stroll through the park, enjoy the newly planted grass and flowers, and embrace the city from an elevated perspective from 7 a.m. to 10 p.m. daily. For 14th Street and 8th Avenue access, take the A, C, E, or L train to 14th Street & 8th Avenue. For 23rd Street and 8th Avenue access, take the C or E train to 23rd Street. Take the 1, 2, or 3 train to 14th Street and 7th Avenue, the 1 train to 18th Street and 7th Avenue, and the 1 train to 23rd Street and 7th Avenue to access various entry points throughout the park.

Want to see where George Washington once drank to forget his woes and celebrate his victories? Well, if his imbibing habits don't hold much interest for you, the location of his favorite watering hole is also where he bid farewell to his troops at the end of the Revolutionary War. Head to *The Fraunces Tavern Museum,* opened by Samuel Fraunces in 1762 as the Queens Head Tavern. The building itself is the oldest building in Manhattan and a national landmark. Fraunces originally intended to showcase his cooking and offered take-out to the neighborhood. Who knows where modern amenities like midnight pizza take-out would be without Fraunces.

In its heyday, the tavern was a hotspot for politics and national leaders who founded the Chamber of Commerce and overheard plenty of impassioned debates during the Revolutionary War. In 1904, the Sons of the Revolution began housing artifacts and displayed them to the public. The museum represents America's struggle for freedom and is the only museum in Manhattan solely devoted to American Revolutionary War history. It's fittingly displayed in a building that saw much of the wartime action of its day and is a keeper of secrets Washington took to his grave.

After a day of touring, head downstairs to the Fraunces Tavern Restaurant for lunch or dinner and a toast to Washington.

The Fraunces Tavern Museum is located at 54 Pearl St. (212-509-3467; www.frauncestavern.com) and is open Monday through Saturday from noon to 5 p.m. Admission runs $10 for adults, $5 for seniors 65 and over, $5 for children ages 6 to 18, and free for children 5 and under. Take the N, R train to Whitehall

## welcome visitors

New York's *Fleet Week* stirs up quite a frenzy of excitement at the end of May each year. Sailors fill the streets, pouring out from ships along the Hudson. I've never seen so many glowing, bleached, white bell-bottoms in one place. They're easy to spot, friendly, and open doors for you. What else could a city with a reputation for being rude and unyielding ever want?

Street, the 4, 5 to Bowling Green, the 1, 9 to South Ferry, or the J, M, Z to Broad Street. Visit www.frauncestavernmuseum.org for more information.

Want to learn trapeze on your New York City travel adventure? Head to Pier 40 in Hudson River Park to **Trapeze School New York** (212-242-TSNY; www.trapezeschool.com) and take a lesson along breathtaking views of the water. Co-founder Jonathan Conant was inspired after a flight at Club Med's popular trapeze school. Despite the idea that flying around on trapezes in New York City may have seemed like a bad business idea, a prime location was secured, permits were surprisingly approved by the city, and the classes began to catch on. Since 2002, Trapeze School New York has been offering classes to all walks of life—from adrenaline seekers to athletes to couch potatoes to the "casual flyer," so most anyone can join. Ages six on up can take beginner through advanced courses in a flying or static trapeze.

Join in a class of ten students to learn knee hangs, catching, aerial conditioning, intense flying workshops, and more. An indoor trapeze center is located at 518 West 30th St.; find it by taking the A, C, E, 1, 2, 3 trains to Penn Station and walking west for about five minutes. The school has also spread to other cities including Boston and Santa Monica.

If you're looking for waterside dining with a historical twist, you can't get much closer than the **Frying Pan** at Pier 66 Maritime in Chelsea. This historic lightship was built in 1929, among only 100 produced, and one of the few remaining. Lightships once served as floating lighthouses to keep their mother ships from running onto rocky ground. Another lightship, the *Ambrose,* is docked at the South Street Seaport Museum and formerly stood at the entrance of New York Harbor.

*The Frying Pan* once housed up to fifteen men, protecting its mother ship, also called *the Frying Pan.* The lightship was eventually abandoned near an oyster cannery before it fell into disrepair and finally sank off the shores of Whitehaven, Maryland. There it spent the next three years resting at the bottom of the Chesapeake Bay before it was rescued and restored. Today, the ship is on the New York State and Federal Registers of Historic Places. Visit www .fryingpan.com or call (212) 989-6363 for more information.

Right next door to the *Frying Pan,* or rather the next boat over, is the **John J. Harvey,** which was one of the most powerful fireboats in service. Built in 1931, the boat pumped out 18,000 gallons of water per minute during its heyday. The boat was retired in 1994 and landed on the National Register of Historic Places in 2000. *John J. Harvey* was bought in an auction in 1999 and eventually moved to Pier 66 Maritime. The owners are known to host infrequent public trips and "harbor displays" periodically. Check fireboat.org for a calendar of upcoming events.

After visiting the *Frying Pan* and the *John J. Harvey* fireboat, take a moment to stroll around **Pier 66 Maritime.** It was once a Delaware, Lackawanna, and Western railroad car float. Built in 1946, the former car float and railroad barge carried railroad cars from New Jersey to New York City. At one time, it rested off Pier 63 and was called Pier 63 Maritime. The pier was eventually anchored to house the historic *Frying Pan* lightship before Manhattan Kayak Company and the *John J. Harvey* took up residence alongside. Get to the barge by taking a C or E train to 23rd Street and take the M23 cross-town bus west and make your way to 26th Street and the Hudson River. Pier 66 Maritime's bar and grill serves up lunch and dinner from noon to 12:30 a.m. daily. Try the cornmeal crusted calamari, Old Bay garlic fries, or steamed littleneck clams. Visit www .pier66maritime.com for more information.

**Pier 54** (62 Chelsea Piers; 212-336-6666; www.chelseapiers.com) near Chelsea offers free movies and concerts in the summer right on the pier with their RiverFlicks and RiverRocks series. I viewed the film *This is Spinal Tap* for the first time in my life against a towering screen silhouetted against the Hudson. This area of Hudson River Park also houses Basketball City, golfing, rock climbing, recreation, outdoor eateries, and more.

Curious what a docked aircraft carrier at Pier 86 is doing along the Hudson River? Its deck is currently showcasing a mismatched collection of planes at the **Intrepid Sea, Air & Space Museum.** In 1943, the *Intrepid* was commissioned during World War II and also served as a recovery vessel for NASA, during the Vietnam War, and during the Cold War. Despite her heroic reputation, she was slotted for the scrap heap. In 1982, a New York real estate developer and a journalist joined forces to save her from destruction and turned the aircraft carrier into a museum and a National Historic Landmark in 1986. Among its collection, visitors can tour the USS Growler, a diesel electric submarine that once patrolled for nuclear activity. Check out one of my favorites, the British Airways Concorde, and learn about its world speed record for passenger airliners when it flew from New York to London in just under three hours. There's also an F-16 Fighting Falcon on duty during Desert Storm, an F-14 Tomcat, F-4 Phantom II, a MiG-15, and much more on display.

The Intrepid Sea Air Space & Museum is located off of 42nd Street on the Hudson River. Hours can vary by season, so check www.intrepidmuseum.org or call 877-957-SHIP for more information. Tickets run $19.50 for adults, $14.50 for seniors 62 and older, $15.50 for veterans and college students with valid ID, $14.50 for children ages 3 to 17, and free for children under 3, retired military, and active duty members. Guided tours are free on a first-come, first-served basis. By train, A, C, E, N, Q, R, S, W, 1, 2, 3, 7, or 9 train to 42nd St.

# Flea Markets

New York City shopping doesn't just end at famous department stores and high-end boutiques. Flea markets are part of the city's tried-and-true tradition, where you can haggle your way to discounts on everything from jewelry to knock-off purses to art to dishes. You can hit up popular markets, or just walk through Soho on a weekend and peruse local vendors who set up shop on their own. My friend visiting from Atlanta asked why the vendors sold purses on the streets so cheaply, if they were fake or hot off the back of a truck. I told her it was probably a little of both. So don't be enraged if you spend $50 on a Prada bag in Chinatown and discover it's a knock-off.

Always try haggling a little, vendors expect it and won't respect you if you don't. The exceptions are used books that are already on sale for a dollar and anything dirt cheap. In that case, just pay full price or they'll disgustedly tell you to leave. Here are a handful of flea markets to check out:

**Annex/Hell's Kitchen Antique Fair**
West 39th Street between 9th and 10th Avenues
www.hellskitchenfleamarket.com/flea market/index.php
Shop for art, antiques, vintage clothing, home décor, jewelry; open Saturday and Sunday, 9 a.m. to 6 p.m.

**Brooklyn Flea**
Fort Greene on Lafayette between Clermont and Vanderbilt at Bishop Loughlin Memorial High School
www.brooklynflea.com

Shop for records, clothes, jewelry, antiques, original artwork, photographs, and frames in two neighborhoods. Every Saturday from 10 a.m. to 5 p.m., seasonally, check Web site for hours and dates.

**Brooklyn Bridge Flea in DUMBO**
Underneath the bridge near River café
www.brownstoner.com/brooklynflea
Look for John Murphy's photographs and exquisite hand-finished frames. Sunday from 11 a.m. to 6 p.m.

Now that you've made your way up the Hudson, jump down east to unravel more of the city's offbeat attractions. Most tourists stick to the bloated area of Canal and Broadway when exploring Chinatown and wade through souvenir shops and food vendors spilling onto the streets and clogging the artery of the neighborhood. Instead, venture further into Chinatown to explore its core, or get a dose of culture at the ***Museum of Chinese in America.*** MOCA was founded in 1980 to preserve the history and culture of Chinese descendents living in the United States. The museum is also positioning itself to be a "cultural anchor" in Chinatown.

The museum thoughtfully blends American and Chinese culture, blurring the lines of interpretation between the two for Chinese-Americans. A historical

### The Garage Indoor Antiques Market

112 West 25th St. between 6th and 7th
Avenues

(212) 647-0707

www.hellskitchenfleamarket.com/flea
market/index.php

Shop for paintings, prints, antiques,
rugs, furniture, silver, and more.
Saturday and Sunday from 9 a.m. to 5
p.m.

### Grand Bazaar

West 25th Street between Fifth and 6th
Avenues

Open year-round, shop for pottery,
textiles, baskets, drums, furniture, art,
jewelry, and standard flea fare. Saturday
and Sunday from 6 a.m. to 6 p.m.

### Greenflea

Columbus Ave between 76th and 77th
Streets

www.greenfleamarkets.com

Find indoor and outdoor market with
imports, handmade crafts, books,
clothes, antiques, farmers' produce.
Sundays from 10 a.m. to 6 p.m.

### Nolita Market

268 Mulberry St.

www.themarketnyc.com

A designer flea market where young
fashion designers double as vendors.
Shop for designer bargains, funky
clothes, pillows, handbags, hats, and
jewelry. Friday, Saturday, and Sunday
11 a.m. to 7 p.m.

### PS 321

7th Avenue between 1st and 2nd
Streets

www.parkslopefleamarket.com

Look for dishes, clothing, art, jewelry,
some antiques, and furniture. Saturday
and Sunday from 9 a.m. to 5 p.m.

### SOHO Antiques Fair

Grand Street and Broadway

Browse for antiques, crafts, clothes, jewelry, and random items. Saturday and
Sunday from 9 a.m. to 5 p.m.

look at culture, immigration, and Chinese living in New York is depicted
through local and international artists. Even if you're not of Chinese descent,
you'll appreciate the Journey Wall. Designed by Maya Lin, who also designed
the Vietnam Memorial in Washington, a series of bronze tiles links Chinese-
American surnames from their origin in China to the American towns they
settled in. The museum itself reminds me of an uncovered Chinese relic gently
renovated and modernized. Lin blended traditional Chinese architecture with
exposed brick, a sky-lit courtyard opening into exhibition galleries, auditorium,
and contemporary touches.

The Museum of Chinese in America (212-619-4785; www.mocanyc.org) is
located at 215 Centre St. and is open from Monday 11 a.m. to 5 p.m., Thursday

11 a.m. to 9 p.m., Friday 11 a.m. to 5 p.m., and weekends 10 a.m. to 5 p.m. Admission runs $7, seniors 65 and older and students with school ID $4, and children under 12 are free. Visit on Thursday for free admission. By train, take the N, R, Q, W, J, M, and 6 trains to Canal Street.

Ninety-seven Orchard Street is the first tenement to be preserved in America, and it is the site of the *Lower East Side Tenement Museum.* The museum's mission is to "promote tolerance through the presentation and inter-pretation of the variety of urban immi-grant experiences on Manhattan's Lower East Side, a gateway to America." The museum also hosts a series of week-end walks through the historic Orchard Street area. "The Streets Where We Lived" helps visitors learn how different immigrant groups shaped, and continue to shape, the Lower East Side.

## freenyc

Though New York may be one of the world's most expensive cities, there are more free things to do in the city than you'll ever possibly have time for. Visit www.freenyc .net to find free movies, concerts, gallery openings, lectures, book signings, wine tastings, and more. Take your own tour of the city's libraries; jazz at St. Peter's church; chamber music at the Julliard School; and lectures and signings by famous authors at bookstores. Just a heads up, you'll find the most free events, concerts, and recreation during summer months when parks open their lawns as a venue.

The museum (212-982-8420; www .tenement.org) is located at 91 Orchard Street and ticket prices run $20 for adults, $15 for students, and $15 for seniors 65 and older. Tours run seven days a week and start at 10:15 a.m. with the last tour at 5 p.m. Take the B or D trains to Grand Street, the F to Delancey Street, or the J, M, or Z to Essex Street.

More Lower East Side history—and an amazing, go-home-and-brag-to-your-friends pastrami sandwich—can be found nearby at *Katz's Deli* at 205 East Houston St. (212-254-2246; www .katzdeli.com). Not only are their sandwiches mouth-watering, but the expan-sive dining room also evokes memories of the neighborhood's good old days, when egg creams cost just a nickel.

Katz's has been around since 1888 when a Russian immigrant family set up shop in one of the poorest neighborhoods in the city. Loyal locals, celebrities, and even former presidents grace the historic, if not unglamorous, dining hall. But tourists may recognize the deli from the infamous, sexy scene between Meg Ryan and Billy Crystal in *When Harry Met Sally.* (My guess is she worked up such a fuss over the sandwiches, and not over her romantic partner in the film.) The deli is open Monday and Tuesday from 8 a.m. to 9:45 p.m., Wednesday and Thursday from 8 a.m. to 10:45 p.m., Friday to Saturday from

8 a.m. to 2:45 a.m., and Sunday 8 a.m. to 10:45 p.m. Take the F or V train to 2nd Avenue.

In 1887, *The Eldridge Street Synagogue* first opened its doors during the High Holiday to accommodate the influx of Jewish immigrants to the Lower East side. From 1880 to 1924, two-and-a-half million Jews from Eastern European countries came to the United States, with an estimated 85-percent settling in New York. Once a thriving religious center for merchants, lawyers, laborers, and a mix of working class, the Jewish population began dispersing further into the Lower East Side and beyond. Eventually the synagogue began to fall into disrepair before the Eldridge Street Project was founded in 1986 to bolster renovation and preservation efforts.

In 1986, *The Eldridge Street Museum* (12 Eldridge St.; 212-219-0302; www.eldridgestreet.org) opened within the synagogue to preserve and honor the culture, history, and traditions of Jewish immigrants in New York's Lower East Side. They give tours, hold services, and parallel their heritage to modern culture.

The museum is open from Sunday through Thursday from 10 a.m. to 5 p.m., with hour-long tours given on the half-hour with the last tour beginning at 4 p.m. Check their Web site for holiday closings and changes in schedules. Ticket prices run $10 for adults, $8 for students and seniors over 62 years old, and $6 for children ages 5 to 18. Get to the museum by taking the F train to East Broadway, the B or D to Grand Street, and the 6, N, or R trains to Canal Street

Discerning shoppers with an eye for emerging trends, and distaste for bargain bins, head to *Inven.tory* (212-226-5292; www.inventorynyc.com) at 237 Lafayette St. and Spring. If you're looking for that feeling of wanting to see and be seen, this place is it. There are high-lofted ceilings, and a DJ spins records while you shop for overstocked items, designer boots, leather hand-bags, jeans, blazers, and a section devoted to vintage clothing. While the concept of buying overstocked merchandise and selling at a steal is the same as Filene's Basement or Century 21, you're more likely to feel Nolita-hip and on the cutting edge of fashion instead of fighting over racks of mangled hangers and crumpled shirts after a heavy day of sales. Inven.tory also prides itself on its eye for selecting only up-and-coming, or arrived, designers. Shop Monday through Saturday noon to 8 p.m. and Sunday 11 a.m. to 7 p.m.

For a look at the history of firefighters in an authentic firehouse, head to 278 Spring St. in Soho to the *New York City Fire Museum.* Currently show-casing the largest collection of fire-related artifacts in the country, the museum features fire engines, antique equipment, and horse-drawn fire trucks. Animal lovers can learn more about the brave fire horses and dogs that served the city over the decades. Check out the display featuring the first FDNY ambulance, which originated to aid injured horses. A fire museum in the city wouldn't be complete without a memorial to the events of 9/11. See over 400 patches left behind by visiting firefighters after the attack. The emotional memorial on the first floor is appropriately supplied with tissue for visitors.

The New York City Fire Museum (212-691-1303; www.NYCFireMuseum .org) is open Tuesday through Saturday from 10 a.m. to 5 p.m. and on Sunday from 10 a.m. to 4 p.m. The museum is closed on Monday and on New Year's Day, Easter Sunday, July 4th, Thanksgiving, and Christmas Day. There is a suggested donation of $5 for adults, $2 for seniors and students, and children under 12 are $1. Take the C or E to Spring Street or the 1 train to Houston Street.

While New York City isn't short on impressive museums dedicated to the preservation of modern and contemporary art, it also has a handful of specialized museums that often go unnoticed. *The Museum of Comic and Cartoon Art* houses a unique collection of comic books, humorous illustration, computer-generated art, graphic novels, videos, and sport cartoons. The museum is small, but long on illustrations and cartoons you may have never heard of before.

Past exhibits included "The Comics of David Mazzucchelli, Peter Kruper, and Irwin Hansen: Heroes to War Orphan." One of its more surprising artifacts is a Nazi boy solder drawn by Mary Stewart, Jimmy Stewart's sister. Classic Warner Brothers fans can take a journey through the collection of rare Bugs Bunny and Daffy Duck drawings.

The Museum of Comic and Cartoon Art (212-254-3511; www.moccany .org) is located at 594 Broadway, Suite 401, and is open Tuesday to Sunday from noon to 5 p.m. Tickets cost $5 for adults, with children 12 and under free. Take the B, D, F, G trains to Broadway/Lafayette Street, and the N or R to Prince Street.

## Like Getting the Keys to the City

The annual **Open House New York** is an off-the-beaten-path traveler's dream. This innovative, and free, weekend features hundreds of tours and events throughout the city. In past years, the organizers convinced the legendary Murray's Cheese to open their aging caves for free, offered a tour of the restored Broad Street Ballroom, took a trip to Harlem's Casa Frela Gallery, and explored Brooklyn's underground **Atlantic Avenue Tunnel Tour.** This event is held every October; visit www.ohny.org/programs for updated dates, information, and reservations.

For low-cost food with flair, head to 6th Street between 1st and 2nd Avenues in the East Village and wait for the onslaught of doormen to beckon you into their brightly decorated restaurants with dripping lights, red shiny wallpaper, and mirrors tacked to the ceiling. They will aggressively invite you to eat at their restaurant just seconds after they watch you walk out the door of their competitors, knowing you're freshly stuffed from your meal. Many of the restaurants are BYOB and typically feature fabulously tacky décor and dangling lights. More upscale options can be found by strolling down Sixth Street and peeking indoors.

While strolling through the East Village, take inventory of your New York City expectations. If you're disappointed that the city seems to have lost its bohemian flavor your aging guidebooks and Woody Allen films evoked, head to *Tompkins Square Park* (Avenues A to B, and East 7th to East 10th Streets; www.nycgovparks.org/parks/tompkinssquarepark) for a thread of that culture you crave. Surrounded by the trendy East Village and Alphabet City, it's still full of both young and old looking for artistic expression and a place to get away from the rising rents and corporate litter in their surrounding neighborhoods. In the 1980s, the park was considered a high-crime area and no one was venturing into its boundaries for real estate investments. A riot even broke out in 1988, which led to its temporary close for renovation. A combination of gentrification in the East Village, new real estate trends, and a park curfew has made it more tourist and hipster friendly. Basketball courts, dog runs, playgrounds, and outdoor chess boards now abound.

If you're disappointed by Tompkins Square Park's increasing gentrified flavor, you can still stop by for the Howl! Festival held annually in the park, along with one of the biggest dog Halloween parties in the United States. Dogs come costumed with their owners to a crowd of several thousand spectators. The park formerly hosted Wigstock, an outdoor drag festival drawing drag queens and transvestites from across the country.

Tompkins Square Park is also home to the city's first dog run, aptly named *First Run* (www.nycgovparks.org/parks/tompkinssquarepark). Dogs wrestle and frolic, mingle with other urban pups and hydrant fountains, and splash in shallow pools during summer. There is also a memorial bone statue where owners put the tags of dogs who have passed on.

For nature lovers, take in the large collection of American elm and weeping willows towering around the park and lining nearby streets. It gives the traditionally bohemian neighborhood a soft and whispery edge. My husband frequently refers to it as the "Savannah, Georgia, District of New York."

Off of Tompkins Square Park on 10th Street near Avenue A lies the *Russian and Turkish Bath House* (268 East 10th St.; 212-674-9250; www

.russianturkishbaths.com). Guests can spend the day in an ice cold pool, steam baths, Russian sauna, redwood sauna, aromatherapy room, outdoor sun deck, and Swedish shower. Massages, Dead Sea salt scrub, black mud treatment, and sports massages are also available. Check the Web site for co-ed, men-, or women-only days. The bath house has operated since 1892 and earned its name from its most popular rooms on site.

As you explore the city, you'll notice neighborhoods turn from toppling apartment complexes to squat row houses to magnificent brownstones on a dime. Unfortunately, most of New York's spectacular brownstones, row houses, and grand homes have been sold off and divided into multiple apartments and consequently renovated into modern dwellings. **The Merchant's House Museum** is the city's last family home preserved intact both inside and out from the 19th century. The home was built in 1832 as a red-brick and white-marble row house and still features the family's original furnishings and possessions dating back before the Civil War.

## pickledayfestival

New York's *Food Museum* (212-966-0191; www.nyfoodmuseum.org/_phome.htm), which has no permanent home, holds an annual Pickle Day Festival. Visitors sample pickles from India, Haiti, and famous kosher dills right from the Lower East Side of Manhattan. You can also snack on pickled items like okra, fish, eggs, limes; take a walking tour; let the kids loose with children's activities; and watch cooking demonstrations.

The Merchant's House Museum (212-777-1089; www.merchantshouse.com) is open on Monday, Thursday, Friday, and weekends from noon to 5 p.m. The museum is closed Easter Sunday, 4th of July, Thanksgiving, Christmas Day, New Year's Eve and Day. Admission runs $8 for adults, $5 for seniors over 65 years old and students. Children under 12 are free when accompanied by an adult. By train, take the N or R to 8th Street, the 6 to Astor Place, or the F or B to Broadway-Lafayette Street.

Tucked away in a basement bar in Greenwich Village, **Marie's Crisis** (59 Grove St.; 212-243-9323) boasts a deliciously sordid history. It opened during the 1850s and has functioned as a prostitute den, a gay bar, and a Prohibition refuge. Gay men, musical theater aficionados, and locals looking for a good time gather at the piano over basic beers and well drinks. The bar was called Marie's, but later the word "Crisis" was added as a nod to Thomas Paine's 1776 pamphlet *The Crisis*. Paine died in a house that was formerly located on the site before the bar was constructed. It is open daily from 5:30 p.m. to 4 a.m. Take the 1 train to Christopher Street, or the A, B, C, D, E, F, and V trains to West 4th St.

# LGBT Community Center

*The Lesbian, Gay, Bisexual and Transgender Community Center,* located in Greenwich Village, is the largest of its kind on the East Coast and second largest in the world. Among the services offered are a free welcome packet with maps and community information; an information and referral staff on duty throughout the center's open hours; and Internet access at the David Bohnett Cyber Center. The center also runs social service, public policy, educational, and cultural/recreational programs. The National Archive of Lesbian, Gay, Bisexual, and Transgender History, also located at the center, sponsors regular exhibits, publications, and scholarly research activities. The Lesbian, Gay, Bisexual, and Transgender Community Center, 208 West 13th St. (212-620-7310; www.gaycenter.org), is open daily from 9 a.m. to 11 p.m.

Nearby Washington Square Park in Greenwich Village, **Blue Hill Farm** (75 Washington Place; 212-539-1776; bluehillfarm.com) is known as a city gem under the culinary leadership of chef Dan Barber, a pioneer in serving fresh, quality food straight from local farms. It was once known as a relatively low-key restaurant until President Barack Obama and First Lady Michelle Obama made an impromptu visit. The restaurant more or less secured a spot directly on the well-worn path with its high-profile patrons. Located in a former speakeasy, this restaurant serves up ingredients in part from Barber's family-owned Blue Hill Farm in the Berkshires. The ingredients are fresh—right down to the beehive producing the restaurant's honey. Try the poached duck or Rabbi Bob's Pastured Veal. Blue Hill Farm is open Monday through Saturday from 5:30 p.m. to 11 p.m. and Sunday from 5:30 p.m. to 10 p.m. By subway, take the F, V, D, B, A, C, or E trains to West 4th Street.

For more casual dining, head to the **Peanut Butter & Co** (240 Sullivan St.; 866-ILOVEPB). The low-key peanut butter shop and eatery sells Fluffernutter, lunchbox specials with fresh peanut butter on apricot preserves, and other peanut-inspired specialties. "The Elvis" features a grilled peanut butter sandwich teaming with bananas and honey with optional bacon. The shop also sells spicy, chocolate, and white peanut butter delicacies. You can also order a straight up classic—peanut butter with grape jelly on bread. The shop is open from 7 a.m. to 11 p.m. daily.

Over at **Murray's Cheese,** lactate tolerant locals pour over every kind of cheese imaginable from appenzeller, asiago pressato, evora, sheep milk, French goat cheese—the list goes on. I might need another guide book to cover the glut of cheese going on over there. You can also find cured meats, breads, nuts, chocolates, olives, and an assortment of mouth-watering specialty

## Get a Taste of the City

Twice a year, once in winter and once in summer, scores of the city's restaurants, including many fine dining and expensive joints, participate in Restaurant Week. For two weeks only, they offer three-course lunches and dinners at bargain prices. Check www.nycvisit.com for details.

foods to go with your cheese selection. The shop offers tasting classes, a tour of the aging cheese caves, and Cheese U Boot camp where the owners proclaim "We're Taking Cheese U To The Next Level." Murray's also teaches patrons how cheese is made, offers basic tastings, explains cheese appreciation, gives demonstrations and lectures, and shows how to talk cheese like you actually know what you're talking about.

The shop is named for a Jewish Spanish civil war veteran and communist, Murray Greenberg. He apparently had a wholesale butter and egg shop on Cornelia Street in 1940, but wasn't afraid to buy cheap cheese, trim it, and sell it for profit. Eventually the shop was sold to his clerk Louis Tudda and in 1985, he took on current partner Rob Kaufelt, aka The Big Cheese. The shop moved and settled on Bleeker Street with another location recently opened in Grand Central. Call 888-MY-CHEESE or visit www.murrayscheese.com for more information.

Take a stroll through historic **Washington Square Park** on Fifth Avenue and Waverly Place between West 4th and MacDougal Streets (www.nycgov parks.org/parks/washingtonsquarepark) on your journey through the West Village. This urban park is one of my most beloved in New York and bristles with street performers, New York University students, artists, musicians, lovebirds, tourists, and professionals both young and old. Take a walk during fall when the leaves are changing and watch strangers strike up an impromptu game of chess at the tables with a chess board painted on the table tops.

The park was named for George Washington and once held the marsh of Manhattan's Minetta Brook. In 1797, the park was used as a public execution ground and potter's field to bury the poor and common laborers. Look for Hangman's Elm on the northwest corner of the park, rumored to be the site of the former hangings. The park also served as a Military Parade Ground before becoming a public park in 1827 and attracting the attention of the city's wealthy. Manhattan's elite began moving into Greek Revival mansions in droves on the northern side of the park. That didn't stop the park from becoming a stomping ground for activists, musicians, and grassroots politics during the '50s and '60s.

The crowning glory of the grounds is easy to spot. The Arch resembling Paris's Arc de Triomphe was erected in 1889 to memorialize the centennial anniversary of George Washington's Presidential inauguration. Stanford White, an esteemed architect of his time, designed it out of wood and papier-mâché. There was so much buzz around it that the city decided to construct a permanent marble one that took six years to complete. Until 1971, traffic actually flowed underneath the arch and, at various points over the years, visitors could venture inside its leg and climb to an observation area. Sit in the park during lunch with a sandwich from a nearby deli for a session in people watching or game of chess. To find the park, take the F, V, B, D, A, C, or E trains to West 4th Street.

A visit to Greenwich Village wouldn't be complete without a stop to appreciate its art scene. New York University's **Grey Art Gallery** is a working university art museum focused on what they call human culture and its social context with art. The gallery stands in what was once A. E. Gallatin's Museum of Living Art, the university's first museum and the first institution in the country that featured work by Picasso, Léger, and Miró. The gallery has kept up the tradition of being first in line to showcase new art. In 2009, they were the first U.S. exhibition to focus on acrylic paintings from the Australian indigenous settlement of Papunya. This lesser-known museum is worth a stop to see seasoned and new artists, photography exhibits, paintings, illustrations, and more.

## ariver**runs** throughit

So what happened to the Minetta Brook that once fed the forgotten marshy area of Washington Square Park? It's still here, flowing below Manhattan. The city was once a tangle of streams some 100 years ago and a lingering holdout, Minetta Brook, flows throughout the bowels of the city. There's a rumor you can still see its evidence in the lobby at 2 Fifth Ave. in Greenwich Village. Look for the odd pipe that reaches down to the depths of the brook. After a storm, locals say water bubbles back up the makeshift fountain.

The Grey Art Gallery (212-998-6780; www.nyu.edu/greyar) is located in New York University at 100 Washington Square East and is open on Tuesday, Thursday, and Friday from 11 a.m. to 6 p.m., on Wednesday from 11 a.m. until 8 p.m., and Saturday from 11 a.m. until 5 p.m. There is a suggested donation of $3 for the public, free to NYU students, faculty, and staff. By subway, take the A, C, E, B, D, F, or V to West 4th Street. Or take the R, W to 8th Street, the 6 to Astor Place.

Buried in the headquarters of Forbes Magazine lobby, the **Forbes Galleries** display the whimsical collection of magnate Malcolm Forbes Jr. Apparently,

# Giving Freeloaders a New Name

Over the years, *freegan* groups have been sprouting up across the country, looking for ways to cut back on their consumer spending by dumpster diving coast to coast. Although the term "freegan" may be new, the concept isn't. New Yorkers have been perusing the streets on trash day for years, picking up pieces of art, coffee tables, electronics, and books. NYU holds one of the most popular freegan and public foraging events—the day students move out. Stories of discarded iPods, designer duds, furniture, books, and more bring out locals in droves to scour the city's leftovers.

The freegan movement in New York holds frequent trash tours, showing curious and aspiring freegans how to safely forage for food, cook a meal, and furnish your apartment. There are also Freegan Bicycle Workshops, Freegan Reading Groups, Grub Community Building Meals, and Urban Foraging 101. Most meetings and tours are free, often with an encouraged donation to the cause. Media often shows up for a story and leaves feeling surprised at how easy and effective a freegan lifestyle can be. Check www.freegan.info for upcoming New York City freegan events.

much of his wealth was spent on amassing toy soldiers, antique games, toy boats, trophies, and Forbes artifacts litter the galleries. One of the more intriguing displays, The Monopoly Exhibit, takes a look back at its origins of a wooden board game called The Landlord's Game from the 1920s complete with a Go to Jail stop.

The Forbes Galleries (212-206-5548; www.forbesgalleries.com) are located at 62 Fifth Ave. and are free to the public from 10 a.m. to 4 p.m. on Tuesday through Saturday. Advance reservations are required on Thursday for groups only. Take the 4, 5, 6, N, R, A, C, E, B, D, 1, or 9 subway trains to 14th Street.

Upstate in Buffalo, the house still stands where Theodore Roosevelt was inaugurated president of the United States. Here in the city you can see where his life began at the Theodore Roosevelt Birthplace National Historic Site. The building standing here today is a faithful reconstruction of the brownstone row house in which Roosevelt was born on October 27, 1858. It was built following the former president's death in 1919, replacing a nondescript commercial building that had gone up only three years before, when the original Roosevelt home was torn down.

Open to the public since 1923, and a National Historic Site since 1963, the reconstructed Roosevelt home is furnished in the same style with many of his original belongings on display. The president's widow and his two sisters supervised the reconstruction of the home, recalling room layouts, furniture placement, and even interior color schemes. The end result deftly blends the life of a scholar and athlete who would later become a rancher, police commissioner, Rough Rider, New York governor, and President of the United States.

The "new" Roosevelt house stands in stubborn contrast to the modern buildings that surround it, reminding us of just how severely the neighborhoods of New York have changed and morphed over the years. The ***Theodore Roosevelt Birthplace National Historic Site*** is at 28 East 20th St. (212-260-1616; www.nps.gov/thrb), and is open Tuesday through Saturday 9 a.m. to 5 p.m.; closed on federal holidays. Admission to the house is free. Tours of the period rooms are available by guided tours only at 10 a.m., 11 a.m., and 1 p.m. By train, take the 6 to Lexington Avenue, or the N and R trains to East 23rd Street and Broadway.

Book lovers find bliss in the expansive collection at the ***Strand Bookstore,*** 888 Broadway (12th Street; 212-473-1452; www.strandbooks.com). With an inventory that includes "18 miles of books," the Strand stocks everything from best sellers to dollar books to rare editions and signed originals that sell for thousands of dollars. The staff is typically well-versed in literary history, emerging authors, and popular favorites. There is also a Strand Annex at 95 Fulton St. and a Central Park kiosk at 60th Street and Fifth Avenue, across the street from the Pierre Hotel.

The Strand Bookstore originally opened in 1927 by Ben Bass after the famous publishing street in London. There were once forty-eight bookstores in all lining New York's "Book Row" running from Union Square to Astor Place built up during the late 1800s. The Strand is a rare sight, a lone survivor in a world once known as a book hub.

The main bookstore on 12th Street is open from Monday to Saturday from 9:30 a.m. to 10:30 p.m., although their Rare Book Room closes at 6:20 p.m. On Sundays, visit Strand from 11 a.m. to 10:30 p.m. Take the N, R, Q, W, 4, 5, 6, or L trains to Union Square. The Central Park kiosk is open 10 a.m. to dusk April through December, although it sometimes closes during inclement weather.

When ***New York City's Museum of Sex*** opened in 2005, locals seemed a little perplexed over what exactly its exhibits would entail. Though it seems fitting such a museum would be housed in this city where anything from Greek Revival mansions to burlesque shows reside within the same borders. To greet its guests at the museum's opening, the inaugural exhibit, "NYCSEX: How New York Changed Sex in America," explored an evolution of sex.

Founder Daniel Gluck designed the museum's mission around the history, evolution, and cultural significance of human sexuality. Its focus is eclectic, ranging from drawings, paintings, photographs, film and video, ancient artifacts, and old and new technology. The Museum of Sex also features guest lectures, seminars, and performance art throughout the year. Their gift store

## ANNUAL EVENTS IN NEW YORK CITY

### JANUARY

**National Black Fine Art Show**
(212) 777-5218
www.blackfineartshow.com

**New York National Boat Show**
(212) 922-1212
www.nyboatshow.com

**Three Kings Day Parade**
Spanish Harlem
(212) 831-7272
www.elmuseo.org

**Winter Antiques Show at Seventh Regiment Armory**
(718) 292-7392
www.winterantiquesshow.com

### FEBRUARY

**Chinese New Year (month changes yearly)**
(212) 484-1222

**Westminster Kennel Club Dog Show**
(800) 455-3647
www.westminsterkennelclub.org

### MARCH

**Greater New York Orchid Show**
www.gnyos.org

**Greek Parade**
(212) 484-1222
www.greekparade.org

**International Cat Show**
(212) 465-6741
www.cfa.org/catlanta

**Manhattan Antiques Triple Pier Expo**
(212) 255-0020

**St. Patrick's Day Parade**
(212) 484-1222

### APRIL

**The Easter Parade**
(212) 484-1222

**Macy's Flower Show**
(212) 494-4495

### MAY

**Cuban Day Parade**
(212) 374-5176

**Fleet Week**
(212) 245-0072
www.fleetweek.com

**Great Five-Boro Bike Tour**
(212) 932-0778

**Ninth Avenue Food Festival**
(212) 581-7217

**Washington Square Outdoor Art Exhibit**
(212) 982-6255

### JUNE

**JVC Jazz Festival**
(212) 501-1390

**Lesbian and Gay Pride Week and March**
(212) 807-7433
www.hopinc.org

may just be the only museum store in the country that sells sex toys next to books, home accents, and provocative clothing. Its holdings include the Ralph Whittington collection of erotica, assembled by a distinguished former curator of a prestigious museum, and artifacts from the nearby Harmony Theater,

Metropolitan Opera in the Parks
(212) 362-6000

Museum Mile Festival
(212) 606-2296
www.museummilefestival.org

Puerto Rican Day Parade
(212) 484-1222

Shakespeare in the Park
(212) 539-8500
www.publictheater.org

JULY

Brooklyn Independence Day Parade
(718) 921-3403

Fourth of July Fireworks Spectacular
(212) 484-1222 or (212) 494-2922

AUGUST

Harlem Week
(212) 484-1222

U.S. Open Tennis Championships
(718) 760-6200
www.usopen.org or www.usta.com

SEPTEMBER

African-American Day Parade
(212) 862-8497

Feast of San Gennaro
(212) 768-9320

New York Film Festival
(212) 875-5050

Pulaski Day Parade
www.pulaskiparade.org

West Indian-American Day Parade
(212) 484-1222 or (718) 625-1515

OCTOBER

Columbus Day Parade
(212) 249-9923

Greenwich Village Halloween Parade
www.halloween-nyc.com

NOVEMBER

Macy's Thanksgiving Day Parade
(212) 484-1222 or (212) 494-2922

New York City Marathon
(212) 423-2249 or (212) 860-4455
www.nyrrc.org

DECEMBER

New Year's Eve in Times Square
(212) 768-1560 or (212) 484-1222
www.timessquarebid.org

Radio City Music Hall's Christmas
Spectacular
(212) 247-4777
www.radiocity.com

Rockefeller Center Tree-Lighting
Ceremony
(800) NYC-VISIT
www.nycvisit.com

formerly known as the Melody Burlesque. Recent special exhibitions have
included offerings such as "Stags, Smokers, and Blue Movies" and "Mapping
Sex in America." The Museum of Sex is located at 235 Fifth Ave. (212-689-6337;
www.mosex.com) and is open Sunday to Friday, 11 a.m. to 6:30 p.m.; Saturday

11 a.m. to 8 p.m.; closed Thanksgiving and Christmas. Admission is $14.50 for adults and $13.50 for students and seniors, plus tax. By subway, take the R or W to 28th Street.

One of my personal treasured cross-sections of New York City is the bustling epicenter of **Union Square** at 14th Street and Broadway. A statue of George Washington stands in its center, overlooking a cross-section of lawns, walkways, benches, and a dog run. Students from NYU pour onto the concrete steps at its south edge and lunch on fare from the nearby Trader Joe's and Whole Foods. During the holidays, seasonal stands sell Christmas ornaments, gifts, handmade scarves, art, jewelry, toys, dishes, and more. Year-round, on Monday, Wednesday, Friday, and Saturday, the Greenmarket Farmers' Market sets up shop outdoors and sells fresh produce, preserves, fresh cut flowers, wine, and organic fare. You'll never be at a lack of street

## NYC Passion: Searching for the Perfect Pizza

It's my personal belief that you can't truly understand, or respect, this city without trying a few slices of its world-famous pies. You will quickly discover that New Yorkers are particular and proud about their pizza, and will fiercely defend their neighborhood favorites as if it were a childhood friend. You would need an entire guidebook to get through the scope and depth of what each pizzeria offers, its historical reference to the city, and the culinary genius it evokes. And thus, confident that every visitor to New York might crave a mouth-watering slice at least once (a day), I include a few favorites.

To many pizza aficionados, the very best was formerly found at Una Pizza Napoletana. Locals grieved when they closed up shop in the East Village. But not to worry, they reopened in Williamsburg as **Motorino.** Even Manhattanites won't think twice about taking the L over to Brooklyn for master pizzaolo Anthony Mangieri's handmade, yeast-free, dough allowed to rise for two days. After topping his creations with the finest ingredients, including fresh buffalo mozzarella, fresh basil, and San Marzano tomatoes, he bakes it in a sizzling wood-burning oven. The result is a pie that's both rich and light, bursting with the flavors of Sicilian sea salt. Follow the scent of fresh pizza to 319 Graham Ave.; www.motorinopizza.com.

Devour a pie at **Totonno's,** a Coney Island establishment dating back to 1924. Today Totonno's has several locations. Two are on 2nd Avenue in Manhattan, one between 26th and 27th Streets (212-213-8800), the other between 80th and 81st Streets (212-213-8800). The other two are in Coney Island (718-372-8606) and Yonkers (914-476-4446).

Another old-timer is **Lombardi's** (212-941-7994) on Spring Street, where the crusts are chewy and charred and the cheese is always creamy.

performers, vendors, and artists sketching in their moleskin notebooks at Union Square.

Before I started digging into the research for this book, I had never heard of the **Rubin Museum of Art** and was surprised to learn it was located in a 70,000-square-foot Chelsea building that Barney's department store formerly occupied. Ritual objects, textiles, paintings, artifacts, and ancient gold sculptures now replace designer handbags. Stepping inside, a winding steel-and-marble staircase journeys through seven floors and years of Himalayan and regional art. Nepalese artifacts including gilt copper Shiva Bhairava masks are on display, authentic bronze statues are still dusted with tikka powder, and endless rows of god and goddess statues created for ritual practice are on show.

I'm a sucker for a museum that turns into a venue by night. On Friday at 6 p.m., the museum café transforms into the **K2 Lounge** with two-for-one

In Brooklyn, pizzerias are numerous, but the pies at **Di Fara** (718-258-1367) consistently please, and the wildly popular **Grimaldi's Pizza** in DUMBO (Down Under Manhattan Bridge Overpass) is considered a local institution. Lines form halfway down the block and guests cram together at communal tables with strangers for the opportunity to devour a coal-fired brick oven pizza.

Also on the list is **Keste Pizzeria** in the West Village at 271 Bleeker St. (212-243-1500; www.kestepizzeria.com). You'll understand the true meaning of an authentic Neapolitan Pizzeria under the guidance of Roberto Caporuscio, born on a dairy farm in Pontinia. He went on to study his craft in Napoli, the birthplace of pizza, and brought his craft to New York, much to the pleasure of locals. Eat anything you can get your hands on, though I'm a fan of the Regina Margherita.

Other favorites include **Tosca Cafe** (718-239-3300) on East Tremont Avenue, and **Full Moon** (718-584-3451) off Arthur Avenue. Staten Islanders are fortunate to claim **Denino's Pizzeria** (718-442-9401) on Port Richmond Avenue—have a bite after a ride on the free ferry.

If you're at a loss of where to start on your pizza education and are currently thinking "I wish there was a tour!" you're in luck. **Scott's Pizza Tours** loops through coveted pizza havens by foot or on bus across the boroughs. Learn about the history of the city and pizzerias block by block. Savor slices at some of the most significant pizzerias in the city, see the sites, and leave with your own Pizza Journal and goody bag. Scott is an esteemed and seasoned expert; he judged some twenty pies for *Pizza Today Magazine*'s International Pizza Expo in 2007. Just don't ask Scott where to find the best pizza in New York; he likens such a request to asking an artist his or her favorite color. Just try the pizza and decide for yourself. Tours start at $33 and last about three hours for walking tours. Bus tours last 4.5 hours and run $55. Visit www.scottszatours.com for more information and tickets.

cocktails during happy hour. After getting a buzz, tour the galleries for free from 7 to 10 p.m., take in a live jazz performance called *Harlem in the Himalayas,* acoustic series, listen to a professional storyteller, or watch a cabaret film screening.

The Rubin Museum of Art is located at 150 West 17th St. (212-620-5000; www.rmanyc.org) is open on Monday from 11 a.m. to 5 p.m., Wednesday 11 a.m. to 7 p.m., Thursday 11 a.m. to 5 p.m., Friday 11 a.m. to 10 p.m., and weekends from 11 a.m. to 6 p.m. The museum frequently provides a "Bring a Friend for Free" coupon located in the Visit Us section of their Web site. The museum is closed Christmas, Thanksgiving, and New Year's Day. The cost is $10 for adults; $7 for seniors, students, and artists with valid ID; college students with valid ID $2; and children under 12 for free. By subway, take the A, C, and E to 14th Street, the 1 to 18th Street, the 1, 2, 3, F, V, L, N, R, Q, W, 4, 5, 6 to 14th Street.

Head west to the Flatiron district and linger at 23rd and Fifth Avenue. Look for the block-long line of New Yorkers waiting patiently (well, patiently for New Yorkers anyway) at a single kiosk. Don't think twice, trust the locals and join the queue to the *Shake Shack.* The rewards are juicy roadside-style burgers, crisp onion rings, hot fries, cold custards, beer, wine, and desserts. Over the years, the Shake Shack has become so popular, that a live Shack Cam reveals the current "Shack-mosphere" so patrons can gauge how long the wait for burgers is. After hours, you can still see the soft glow of the lamps lighting up the park.

While you're munching on burgers and fries, also digest the fact that some say *Madison Square Park* is where baseball was born after Alexander Cartwright founded the New York Knickerbockers, the first baseball club, in 1845 in the park. It also housed the arm and torch of the Statue of Liberty for nearly six years in hopes of bolstering support and raising funds for her construction. Despite the park's famed history, it fell into nearly complete disrepair by the 1990s before a campaign was launched to secure funds for renovations. Today you can enjoy a burger on the lawn, or join one of the many events including watching the annual U.S. Open live on a big screen.

The Shake Shack (www.shakeshack.com) and Madison Square Park are located between 23rd Street and 26th Street along Fifth Avenue and Madison Avenue. There's also an Upper West Side Shake Shack location at 366 Columbus Ave. Take the R or W to 23rd Street.

Looking for New York Fifth Avenue fashions at a fraction of the cost? You can spend some time looking for flyers advertising sample sales, or just head over to the shop *Vogue* called "The highest quality thrift shop in New York." The *New York City Opera Thrift Shop* carries clothing for men and

## Over and Underground

When not exploring New York on foot (or splurging on a taxi), visitors use the services of the MTA, the most efficient and economical way to get around. The MTA is a vast transportation network, the largest in North America. It currently houses 8,767 rail and subway cars, 6,300 buses, 2,056 miles of tracks, 3,912 bus route miles, and 734 subway stations. Be one of the 8,739,680 weekday riders. Note that visitors with disabilities can ride the buses, which have wheelchair lifts located near the middle of the vehicles. Visit www.mta.org for maps and info, or use the local favorite www.hop stop.com to plan your route from stop to stop. You can also rely on a New Yorker to tell you where to go; locals have pride in mastering the maze of subway lines and will know which lines tend to be delayed, which rarely run on weekends, and shortcuts to your coveted attractions.

The subway network does not service Staten Island, but there is a ferry that runs between Whitehall Street in lower Manhattan and St. George on Staten Island. Though the ferry exists to transport commuters, it offers visitors a 5-mile, twenty-five-minute ride with majestic views of New York Harbor. The ride is also free, so it's a perfect spot to let your feet and wallet recover after a few days on the town. Visit www.siferry.com for details.

women, designer shoes, furniture, household items, and even art. Shop with a cause, as the proceeds go to the costumes for the opera. Not only are goods tax deductible, but donators can receive up to a $10 taxi fare reimbursement. The thrift shop also hosts a Fall Preview with second-hand designs from Marc Jacobs, Valentino, Christian Dior, Armani, Donna Karan, Hugo Boss, Betsey Johnson, and others.

The thrift shop is located at 222 East 23rd St. (212-684-5344; www.nyc opera.com/aboutus/thriftshop.aspx) and is open Monday through Friday from 10 a.m. to 7 p.m. and on Saturday from 10 a.m. to 6 p.m. and Sunday noon from 5 p.m. Take the R train to 23rd Street.

After making a haul on fashions on the cheap, stop at the *Museum at FIT* for a collection dedicated to corsets, costumes, international fashion, fabrics, and couture. The whole scene is enough to make your head explode while rethinking your fashion choices or wondering what women in generations past were possibly thinking. The museum houses the only permanent fashion history exhibit in the country at the Fashion and Textile History Gallery with some 200 pieces and artifacts representing over 250 years of fashion. Low lights hover over the exhibits to protect the textiles, although you may feel like you're looking at a piece of undiscovered history, unearthed from a time capsule of New York fashion.

Despite living in one of the epicenters of fashion, I'm not exactly on the cutting edge or competing with my fellow urban fashionistas. But what I like about the museum is the social, cultural, and historical context it puts the pieces in. Denim will take on a whole new meaning for even a casual observer. You can also see a collection of FIT student work on the main floor. Study the collection that alternates from seemingly garish to exquisite and wonder if any of the names will one day become a household label. Unlike any of the other couture display in Manhattan, admission to the museum is free year-round.

The Museum at FIT is located at 7th Avenue and 27th Street. Hours run Tuesday through Friday from noon to 8 p.m. and Saturday from 10 a.m. to 5 p.m. The museum is closed on legal holidays. By subway, take the 1, A, C, E, F, N, R, or V to the 18th Street Station or the A, C, E, F, or V to 23rd Street. Visit www.FITnyc.edu or call (212) 217-4558 for more information.

I recently discovered the impressive collection of out of print, rare, and popular jazz collection at **The Jazz Record Center** in Chelsea. Buzz up to the eighth floor and wait for the staff to let you in, all the while feeling like you're discovering a secret no one else has uncovered. Jazz lovers can easily spend the entire day lost in a maze of LPs, CDs, 78s, books, videos, T-shirts, jazz books, and magazines. You'll also find a cross-section of blues peppered throughout the shelves. Browse through the maze of jazz or come ready with a list in hand and ask for assistance from the knowledgeable staff.

The Jazz Record Center (212-675-4480; www.jazzrecordcenter.com) is located at 236 West 26th St., Room 804. Stop in on Monday through Saturday from 10 a.m. to 6 p.m. To get there, take the 1 to 28th Street. If you've got a penchant for jazz and want more, try a tour with **Big Apple Jazz Tours**

## A Laughing Matter

If you didn't luck out with coveted lottery tickets for *Saturday Night Live* back in August (the only time you can enter to win them online), head to the **Upright Citizens Brigade** instead. A sketch-comedy favorite among city locals and talent scouts, the Brigade was founded by comedians Amy Poehler, Matt Besser, Ian Roberts, and Matt Walsh after moving their act from Chicago. Tickets run about $10 no matter who is performing—a student from an Improv class or comedy alums Robin Williams, Will Ferrell, Alec Baldwin, Tina Fey, and Mike Myers to name a few. Upright Citizens Brigade students are often recruited by *Saturday Night Live, 30 Rock, The Office,* and *The Daily Show with Jon Stewart.* It is located at 307 W. 26th St.; take the C or E train to 23rd Street. For an updated list of shows, call (212) 366-9176 or visit www .ucbtheatre.com.

## Taxi Tips

Yellow medallion cabs are the only authorized taxis in New York City. There are more than 12,000 yellow medallion cabs in the city, driven by cabbies from some eighty-five different nations. If the cab's center roof light is not lit, it's not available.

One fare covers all passengers. The fare starts at $2.50 for the first 1/5 mile, 40 cents for each 1/5 mile thereafter, and 40 cents for each minute in slow traffic or not in motion. A $1 surcharge is added to rides begun between 4 and 8 p.m., and a 50-cent surcharge is added between 8 p.m. and 6 a.m. Bridge or tunnel tolls are paid by the passenger. Cabs can issue printed receipts, which are especially useful if you leave something behind or need to business expense your trip. There's a flat rate of $45 plus tolls and tip (generally 15 to 20 percent) to transport passengers between Manhattan and John F. Kennedy Airport.

If you've wondered why New York's cabs are yellow, it's because John Herz, who founded the Yellow Cab Company in 1907, chose the color after he read a study by the University of Chicago indicating that it was the easiest to spot.

(718-606-8442; www.bigapplejazz.com). Tour through the jazz haunts of Harlem, explore the Birdland and Village Vanguard clubs, try a Greenwich Village Jazz tour, or ask for a customized tour.Is it possible to tour a building that no longer exists? Well, sort of. If the building is **Pennsylvania Station**—not the dreary modern terminal that crouches beneath Madison Square Garden, but the mighty neoclassical edifice that the Pennsylvania Railroad and McKim, Mead, and White built in 1910 to evoke the Baths of Caracalla and stand, perhaps, for centuries. Demolished barely more than fifty years later in what the *New York Times* declared a "monumental act of vandalism," the old Penn Station was nevertheless too deeply embedded in the sinews of Manhattan to have disappeared altogether. Like the Roman edifices that inspired it, its ghostly fragments lurk beneath its modern successor; see them when you take the 34th Street Partnership's Penn Station Tour, a ninety-minute walk through time that reveals the physical remains of what was once, along with still-glorious Grand Central Station, one of the grand entrances to New York City.

You'll see the pink granite and herringbone brickwork that once paved the station's carriage drive peeking through fake modern tile; discover the last of the iron-and-brass staircases that preceded escalators as a means of accessing the train platforms; stand opposite the only remaining original elevator cage; and look down at a patch of the original glass bricks that allowed sunlight to filter from the upper levels of the station to the tracks below. Along the way, architectural historian John Turkeli will tell the story of the rise and demise of the New York terminus of "The Standard Railroad of the World." To make reservations and learn more, call (212) 719-3434 or visit www.34thStreet.org.

Where can you find Picasso, Bob Dylan, Mozart, Rembrandt, Gutenberg Bibles, and Barbar the elephant all in one place? (Because I know you were hoping to find such a spot.) Try ***The Morgan Library and Museum.*** It's stuffed with what's called "one of the world's great collections" of music, art, literary pieces, period paintings, and modern marvels. Rich people seem to have eccentric tastes around this city, so it's no big surprise that the museum first started as the private library for the exclusive use of Pierpont Morgan, who eventually became one of the greatest cultural benefactors in our country. Pierpont was said to have kicked off his collection around 1890 with historical manuscripts, rare books, paintings, and prints. It was his son, J. P. Morgan Jr., or Jack, who paused to take a look at all those rare finds tucked away in a Renaissance-style palazzo library and realized it was all far too important for private use. He decided to grant his now deceased father's wish to make the collection available to the public, one of the great cultural gifts in our country's history.

Although the Morgan campus has been expanded and renovated, you can still see the original Morgan residence now used as a gift shop and dining hall. Dining room would hardly do it justice. My husband and I eat dinner at a drop-leaf table in our kitchen in Cobble Hill, Brooklyn; while the Morgan's dined in a room that is big enough to fit my entire apartment—and then some. As you wander through the original library full of walnut bookcases stretching up to the room's 30-foot ceilings, look to the bookcase on the left of the entry- way to locate a hidden staircase. I personally fell in love with the Morgans' study, with its deep red walls, ornate carved ceilings, fireplace, and artwork from Pierpont's original collection. I was ready to curl up on the red couch with the Gutenberg Bible and call it a day.

## it's cold in the wild west

If it's your first time in New York, it's likely you'll head to Times Square and pass the Naked Cowboy, a loyal and reliable fixture in the city. Clad in only underwear, a cowboy hat, and boots, he enter- tains crowds year-round with his guitar, rain or shine. He can be found frequenting delis for hot cof- fee throughout the winter, when he is still scantily clad without a coat.

The Morgan Library and Museum is located at 225 Madison Ave. at 36th Street (212-685-0008; www.themorgan.org) and is open Tuesday through Thursday from 10:30 a.m. to 5 p.m., Friday 10:30 a.m. to 9 p.m., Saturday 10 a.m. to 6 p.m., and Sunday 11 a.m. to 6 p.m. Admission costs $12 adults, $8 children under 16, $8 seniors 65 and over, $8 students with current ID, and free for children under

# Simply Brill-iant Music

A few blocks from Times Square Center is the **Brill Building** at 1619 Broadway and 49th Street. Upon first glance, it resembles an ornate building plated with gold and a long lobby with ornate chandeliers and mirrored walls. The building was named for the Brill Brothers who owned a clothing store on the street level and later bought the building from developer Abraham E. Lefcourt. Above the door and near the roof of the building, you can see a bust of a young Alan Lefcourt, the developer's son who died in a crash as a teenager.

The Brill Brothers planned to rent office space to brokers and bankers, but the Depression squashed all financial plans and they started renting to music publishers. There is a sub-genre of pop music referred to as the Brill Sound, with a box set named after it. Chart topping tunes included "Loco-Motion," "Hanky Panky," "Calendar Girl," "One Fine Day," "Chapel of Love," and "Take Good Care of My Baby"—all were birthed inside the building. Phil Spector and Paul Simon were some of the legendary writers who penned their hits inside the building. Today the building is full of offices, including Broadway Video, founded by Lorne Michaels from *Saturday Night Live,* and Broadway Across America.

12 with a paying adult. You can take a free tour at 2 p.m. on weekdays for an overview of the museum and the Morgans, and if you're on a budget, show up on Friday from 7 p.m. to 9 p.m. for free admission. By subway, take the 6 to 33rd Street; the 4, 5, 6, or 7 to Grand Central, or the B, D, F, Q to 42nd Street.

While tourists are known to flock to the **TGI Friday's** at 1552 Broadway in Times Square, few realize they're stepping into a historical vault. The building was once Israel Miller's shop, a skilled shoemaker supplying shoes for Broadway blockbusters. After lunch at present day TGIFridays, look up at the restaurant wall along 46th Street for the four statues of 1920s Broadway actors, including Drew Barrymore's aunt Ethel dressed as Ophelia, Mary Pickford, and Rosa Ponselle.

Nestled in Times Square lies a hidden restaurant even locals miss. At 324 West 46th St., walk up the brownstone steps without bothering to look for a sign, because you won't find one. First-timers are always afraid they're about to walk into someone's home, but upon stepping inside, the maitre de of **Bar Centrale** (212-581-3130; www.barcentralenyc.com) greets guests. A favorite with theater crowds, Broadway producers, and actors, the bar serves small plates, appetizers, mixed drinks, beers, and cocktails. Though pricey for travelers on a budget, it's a quiet place to enjoy a drink before a show or unwind after a day of exploring on foot. You'll feel like you've discovered a secret hideaway.

## Ticket Discounts

Look for the line at for **TKTS** under the "red steps" at Father Duffy Square on 47th Street and Broadway for half-price tickets to Broadway shows. Tickets are available Monday and Wednesday through Saturday, 3 p.m. until 8 p.m.; Tuesday from 2 p.m. to 8 p.m.; and Sunday from 3 p.m. until one half-hour before curtain time. For matinee tickets, on Wednesday and Saturday, tickets are sold between 10 a.m. and 2 p.m. and Sunday 11 a.m. to 3 p.m. There are no evening performance tickets sold from 10 a.m. to 2 p.m. at this location.

A second, and usually less crowded, TKTS booth sits downtown, at the South Street Seaport, 199 Water St., at the corner of Front and John Streets. Purchase same-day evening and next-day matinee performances from Monday to Saturday 11 a.m. to 6 p.m., and Sunday 11 a.m. to 4 p.m.

A third location in downtown Brooklyn can be found at 1 Metro Tech Center at the corner of Jay Street and Myrtle Avenue Promenade. Look for same-day tickets to evening performances, and matinee tickets the day before performances Tuesday to Saturday 11 a.m. to 6 p.m. (This booth is closed for lunch from 3 to 3:30 p.m.) You can also find discounts to Brooklyn performing arts events in addition to Broadway shows. For more information about any of the TKTS locations, visit www.tdf.org.

Wondering what happened to the gritty nightlife, peepshows, and burlesque of Times Square past? It's mostly gone and faded away, replaced by fast food chains, theater haunts, and souvenir shops. But you can still see a throwback to nostalgic burlesque infused with modern flourishes at the city's oldest running variety burlesque show, *Le Scandal.* The show gives a nod to neo-burlesque and vaudeville gone awry, with a "dash of Coney Island." It's not unusual to see a striptease, low brow humor, magic tricks, scantily clad performers of questionable gender, fan dancing, or sideshow acts all in one night. While outrageously tacky, it's not uncommon to see celebrities in the audience mixed in between bachelorette parties and slightly stunned tourists. Le Scandal is, for better or worse, a captivating New York institution.

The venue recently moved from the Cutting Room to the downstairs at West Bank Cafe in the Laurie Beechman Theater at 407 West 42nd St. Tickets run about $25 and shows start at 10:30 p.m., check their Web site at www .lescandal.com or call (212) 388-2988 for updated show information.

If you have daughters, the *American Girl Place* at 609 Fifth Ave. and 49th Street (877-247-5223; www.americangirl.com) probably already sits at the top of your attractions list. The store is packed on weekends with little girls, mothers, and women shopping for new dolls. Birthday parties require a spot on a coveted, and lengthy, waiting list. But you may be unaware that there is also an American Girl Salon on the premises where dolls line up for hours to get their hair professionally styled, ears pierced, and otherwise "dolled up." Take the B, D, F, or V to 47th Street and Rockefeller Center or the E and V trains to Fifth Avenue and 53rd Street.

Walk over to the **Port Authority** (625 8th Ave.; www.panynj.gov) and look for an eight-foot tall bronze statue of Jackie Gleason standing under the overhang to the terminal. Although out in the open and ready to greet visitors, he's easy to miss with the rush of foot traffic coming in and out of the station. Wearing his *Honeymooner's* bus driver's uniform and holding a lunch pail, Jackie watches over 8th Avenue with a smile on his face. His plaque reads, "Jackie Gleason as Ralph Kramden Bus Driver—Raccoon Lodge Treasurer—Dreamer. Presented by the People of TV Land." TV Land has commissioned other statues including Jeannie from *I Dream of Jeannie*.

Head over to **Bryant Park** (www.bryantpark.org) at 42nd Street and 6th Avenue and sit along the tightly manicured lawn to soak up the view of surrounding skyscrapers blanketing the expanse of the park. Grab a coffee and sandwich from a vendor and sit near the fountain on a hot summer day. Once a potter's field and wilderness spot, the city created a man-made lake and pedestrian area called Reservoir Square during the 1800s. The park was surrounded by 50-foot high and 25-foot thick granite walls topped with public promenades.

Today, the park is an urban oasis for visitors looking for a place to relax or catch a free show. On Monday at sunset during the summer, free movies play near the fountain. Come early to find a seat, or standing room, the park fills up fast. The park also houses a working carousel, Le Carousel, a piano, and, during winter months, holiday kiosks and free ice skating (rentals are available for a fee). I would be remiss if I didn't point out that this park has some of

## Waldorf's Secret Station

While window shopping along Park Avenue and 49th, take a moment to take in the infamous **Waldorf Astoria** (100 East 50th St.; 212-355-3100; www.waldorfastoria .com), a New York celebrity in her own right. While you may recognize the hotel as the set of movies and the childhood home of Paris Hilton, the Waldorf harbors a deep secret. Underneath the building lies a secret station marked as Track 61 on Grand Central blueprints. The station sits among the hidden network of passageways and tunnels at Grand Station that are now inaccessible to the public. The station underneath the Waldorf was used by Franklin D. Roosevelt to get to and from New York and safely to his hotel room.

the best public restrooms in the city. The restrooms are clean, regularly maintained, and often have a fresh vase of flowers sitting on a table at its entrance. To reach the park, take the F, V, D, B, or 7 trains to 42nd Street–Bryant Park.

Adjacent to Bryant Park is the **New York Public Library** (455 Fifth Ave.; 212-340-0866; www.nypl.org). The largest marble structure ever attempted in the country during its time, the foundation was laid in 1902. One million books were set aside for its opening some sixteen years later, housed in a stunning Beaux-Arts design building that would rival some of the world's most prestigious architecture. While the library may be familiar to tourists, step inside to see the McGraw Rotunda on the third floor to discover arched ceilings, Corinthian walnut pilasters, and 17-feet high murals depicting the evolution of the written war. Moses carrying down tablets from the mountain is one of the murals on display. If you're short on cash and time, a free visit to the public library is akin to briefly stepping into one of the city's premier museums. The library is open Monday through Thursday 8 a.m. to 11 p.m., Saturday 10 a.m. to 6 p.m., and Sunday 10 a.m. to 6 p.m. Take the F, V, D, B, or 7 trains to 42nd Street and Bryant Park to access the library.

## birdbrainedidea

During 2003, hawks were employed in an effort to scare off menacing pigeons overrunning Bryant Park. Majestic hawks could be seen sweeping through the park, and occasionally buzzing locals. Unfortunately, the program was quickly grounded after a hawk made off with a Chihuahua, most likely mistaking it for a rat. The owner and dog were whisked away to a vet and recovered.

Shutterbugs converge upon the **International Center of Photography** to see one of the largest collections of historical and modern photographs with over 100,000 original prints. The center's permanent collection showcases American and European documentary photos from the 1930s through the '90s. You can also see photographs from magazines between World War I and II including *LIFE*.

While there, check out the Mexican Suitcase and unravel its mysterious origins. In 2007, three cardboard boxes were tracked down in Mexico City and sent to the center. Inside, the staff was startled to find Spanish Civil War negatives by Robert Capa. The surviving negatives had been a mere rumor after their disappearance from his Paris studio at the onset of World War II. In all, 126 rolls of film were discovered, including work by Gerda Taro and David Seymour. Photos ranged from French internment camps for Spanish refugees in 1939 to People's Army training in Valencia to the destruction from the Battle of Teruel. No one really knows how the negatives ended up in Mexico City, although there are reports of the photographer's work showing up in unexpected places before. The center does know the negatives were discovered in General Aguilar's belonging by a Mexican filmmaker named Benjamin Tarver. He apparently inherited it from his deceased aunt, a friend of the general.

The International Center of Photography is located at 1133 Avenue of the Americas at 43rd Street and is open Tuesday through Thursday 10 a.m. to 6 p.m., Friday 10 a.m. to 8 p.m., and weekends from 10 a.m. to 6 p.m. The museum is closed on Monday, New Year's Day, 4th of July, Thanksgiving Day, and Christmas Day. Admission runs $12 for adults, $8 for students and seniors, and children under 12 are free. There is a voluntary contribution on Friday from 5 to 8 p.m. Visit www.icp.org or call (212) 857-0000 for more information.

While Midtown Manhattan may feel like it's all just glass and steel, at the **American Folk Art Museum** the homey and handmade are cherished too. Founded by a group of collectors in 1961, the museum is devoted to preserving the country's rich folk heritage. Its expansive collection includes paintings, drawings, sculpture, textiles, furniture, functional and decorative arts, photographs, and contemporary environmental works. With pieces dating from the mid-eighteenth century to the present, the collection reflects the museum's increasingly broad definition of the field of folk art. The museum presents special exhibitions and events throughout the year and publishes *Folk Art* magazine, the only publication in the country covering the growing field of American folk art.

The American Folk Art Museum is located at 45 West 53rd St. (212-265-1040; www.folkartmuseum.org) and is open Tuesday through Sunday from 10:30 a.m. to 5:30 p.m. and Friday 10:30 a.m. to 7:30 p.m. Admission runs $9 adults, $7 students and seniors, and free for children under 12. If you're on a budget, stop by Friday after 5:30 p.m. and get in free. By subway, take the B, D, F, or V to Rockefeller Center or E to Fifth Avenue/53rd Street. There is also branch location, the Eva and Morris Field Gallery, at 2 Lincoln Square.

Looking for an unusual souvenir? Perhaps the horn of an impala (*Aepyceros melampus*), the skeleton of the

## historyfound allover

Over near the United Nations, a piece of Germany's history can be seen right in New York City. Since its fall in 1989, pieces of the **Berlin Wall** have been donated to various institution and cities, and a few pieces are found within the city. One piece of the Berlin Wall can be found at the entrance to the Intrepid Sea, Air & Space Museum, another in Battery Park City, and one more on 53rd Street between Fifth and Madison Avenues. Washington D.C., Seattle, Los Angeles, and Dayton, Ohio, are just a few of the other U.S. locations with a piece of the historic Berlin Wall.

lookdown fish (*Selene vomer*), or the skull of a tokay gecko will do. **Maxilla &**
**Mandible, Ltd.,** the world's only osteological store, is a natural-history and science emporium with 19,000 square feet of showroom, laboratory, workshop,
and storage facilities. All of their specimens are unique, anatomically accurate,
and obtained from legal and ethical sources. They're at 451 Columbus Ave.
(212-724-6173; www.maxillaandmandible.com), and are open Monday through
Saturday 11 a.m. to 7 p.m. and Sunday 1 to 5 p.m. Closed on major holidays.

Gadget geeks and families can make their way to the **Sony Wonder**
**Technology Lab** under the guise of wanting to take the kids. Here you can
freely play with robots, 3-D animations, and perform faux open-heart surgery
with the help of hepatic technology. Interactive exhibits called *"How Devices*
*Work," "Nanotechnology,"* and *"Robot ZoneFour"* fill four floors and nearly
14,000 square feet. Film screenings, sci-tech workshops, and family workshops
are also available. While admission is free, lines are long and reservations
are required, though the lab does hold a limited amount of walk-up tickets.
There is also an unlimited amount of Sony advertising and devices stuffed in
the walls of every exhibit; it seems like a fair trade for free hands-on use of
up-and-coming technology. There's also a Sony Style retail store, with plenty
of gadgets and toys for adults to buy and take home.

The Sony Wonder Technology Lab is located at 550 Madison Ave. The
lab is open Tuesday through Friday 10 a.m. to 5 p.m. and Sunday noon to 5
p.m. and is closed on Monday and major holidays. By subway, take the 4, 5,
6, N, or R to 59th and Lexington, the E and V to Fifth Avenue, or the F to 57th
Street. Visit www.wondertechlab.sony.com or call (212) 833-8100 for more
information.

If you've already been to a show at the renowned Lincoln Jazz Center,
visit the **Nesuhi Ertegun Jazz Hall of Fame.** The hall's namesake, Nesuhi
Ertegun, was an advocate for jazz and the son of the former Turkish Ambassador to the United States. It was through his father's job that the family settled
in Washington, D.C., and Nesuhi was introduced to soul, jazz, and R&B and
frequented the Howard Theater. He eventually moved to Los Angeles in 1944
to run the Jazzman Record Shop before founding his own label called Crescent
Records where he recorded the Jelly Roll Morton and many others. After building a reputation in the jazz work, Nesuhi joined Atlantic Records in 1956 and
built the label's jazz collection with such greats as John Coltrane, Ray Charles,
and Herbie Mann. Nesuhi also holds the distinction of teaching the country's
first accredited course in jazz at UCLA and being inducted into the Rock and
Roll Hall of Fame in 1991.

To be inducted, over 100 musicians, scholars, and educators from seventeen different countries nominate and select artists who have contributed

## Exploring Roosevelt Island

*Roosevelt Island,* formerly Blackwell's Island, is a 147-acre island sitting in the middle of the East River. Its juxtaposition gives it the unique distinction of being close to the city, yet isolated from the bustle of urban life. Movies like *Dark Water* with Jennifer Connelly set up shop to film and capture that sense of alienation. The island has a depressing past: it was formerly home to a Smallpox Hospital, prison, almshouse, insane asylum, and a city hospital at various points before becoming a quiet, residential neighborhood with grand views of the city. Many tourists and locals simply visit out of curiosity, or to take the only tram in the city. Sitting 250 feet above the East River, the tram runs about every 15 minutes and costs the same as a ride on the subway. It provides a spectacular, and cost-effective, view of the city.

If you're up for a bit of exploring, look to the north end of the island for the Blackwell Island Lighthouse. The 50-foot-tall, octagonal-shaped, Gothic-style lighthouse was built in 1872. The Coast Guard never controlled the lighthouse, rather it was commissioned by the city to light up the insane asylum for boats making their way through what was once known as Hell Gate waters. James Renwick Jr., best known for his work on St. Patrick's Cathedral, designed the lighthouse and New York's institutionalized convicts helped build it. It was in use until the 1940s and became a city landmark in the 1970s.

Take the F train to Roosevelt Island, or head to 59th Street and 2nd Avenue in Manhattan to opt for a ride on the tram (www.rioc.com).

to the development of jazz. Inductees John Coltrane, Count Basie, Miles Davis, Charlie Christian, and Duke Ellington are just a handful who made the cut.

The Nesuhi Ertegun Jazz Hall of Fame (212-258-9800; www.jalc.org/halloffame) is located at 60th Street and Broadway in the Frederick P. Rose Hall at the Lincoln Center. Admission is free, and it is open Tuesday through Sunday from 10 a.m. to 4 p.m. Take the A, B, C, D, or 1 subway trains to 59th Street-Columbus Circle.

While most of the city's museums showcase paintings and sculptures, there is an entire gallery devoted to the art of illustration over at the *Society of Illustrators* at 128 East 63rd St. between Park and Lexington. The society was founded in 1901 by a group of nine artists and a businessman to sit around and discuss art, illustration, and pat each other on the back for their many talents. Monthly dinners were held to feature illustrations and art in the carriage house of William P. Read, J. P. Morgan's personal secretary (or a lawyer in today's terms). Considering how voluminous J. P.'s family collection was (now housed at the Morgan Library and Museum), I wonder if he considered his secretary's pursuit a modest and cute little venture. Club members can still dine on the third floor of the building and sip cocktails while discussing the latest in illustration.

Today's on-site museum houses over two thousand original illustrations in a carriage house built in the 1850s. You can still see memorabilia on display from the days of the artistic founding fathers, temporary exhibits, posters from decades past, and photographs. Gallery hours run 10 a.m. to 8 p.m. on Tuesday, 10 a.m. to 5 p.m. Wednesday through Friday, and noon to 4 p.m. on Saturday. Take the F train to the Lexington Avenue and 63rd Street. Call (212) 838-256 or visit societyillustrators.org for more information.

Tucked away in Central Park lies the *Swedish Marionette Theatre* (79th Street and West Drive; 212-988-9093; www.cityparksfoundation.org/index1. aspx?BD=17009). The cottage was built in 1876 for the Centennial Exposition in Philadelphia. Famed Central Park designer Frederick Law Olmsted moved the model schoolhouse to the park the following year. But it wasn't until the 1990s that the City Parks Foundation finally restored the building and opened it for public use. Today, children can watch marionette and puppet shows or celebrate birthdays in a private party room on the premises.

After you've got the kids captivated by puppets and marionettes, take them to the *Central Park Zoo* and *Friedsam Memorial Carousel.* Although not as impressive as the Bronx Zoo, I actually prefer the park's quaint little zoo. I love taking a leisurely two-hour tour past the resident snow monkeys, polar bears, and birds, and hang out for the sea lion feedings. There's also a penguin and puffin exhibit, an indoor rain forest, and plenty of wildlife to see. I've yet to spot the elusive red pandas, Goodwin and Jen, who spend their time sleeping and hiding out in the exhibit's trees. Among my least favorite residents is the deer mouse. Although perfectly cute and polite, the idea of an animal resembling a rat with long, limber legs is discomforting in a city known for its overzealous rodent population.

As you walk through the exhibits, did you notice an extra something? New York's city ducks can be found sleeping with the otters and quacking at the excitable sea lions, completely oblivious you paid to see snow leopards, not watch them totter through the zoo grounds.

The zoo (www.centralparkzoo.com) is located at 64th Street and Fifth Avenue and hours run Monday through Friday from 10 a.m. to 5 p.m., and weekends and holidays from 10 a.m. to 5:30 p.m. from April 4 until November 1; and daily from 10 a.m. to 4:30 p.m. in winter from November 2 to April 2. General admission runs $10 for adults, $5 for children, and $7 for seniors.

Up next, the Friedsam Memorial Carousel has been in operation since 1871 and was originally powered by a poor, blind horse and his sidekick, a mule. Today's carousel was made by the Stein & Goldstein Company in 1908 to serve as a trolley terminal near Coney Island. A fire and various mishaps occurred, and eventually the carousel was moved to Central Park in 1951. The present one is home to the largest hand-carved figures ever constructed and are all hand painted. I would prefer to report that I rode the carousel by myself, a grown woman, strictly for guide research. But I'll confess that I rode it long before I ever became a travel writer; simply because it looked so inviting and magical from the outside.

You can find the carousel at the 6th Avenue entrance near 59th Street and tickets are a steal at just $1. The carousel (www.centralparkcarousel.com) is open for rides every day from 10 a.m. to 6 p.m. from April through summer and 10 a.m. through dusk during winter, weather permitting, and is also open on major holidays.

Mix a space odyssey, historical journey, and film in one place: located adjacent to the American Museum of Natural History, *The Hayden Planetarium, Rose Center for Earth and Space* holds an impressive technological Space Theater in the upper half of an 87-foot sphere. In the bottom half lies the Big Bang Theater with a four-minute film about how the universe was born. If you know what a customized Zeiss Mk IX Star Projector is, well, you must have been to the planetarium before or have been coveting a glance at one of the dazzling space shows.

When you settle in, you may feel like you accidentally just sat down in the front row of a movie theater as you crane your neck to look at the show above. But as the lights dim and you're hurtled through space, you'll hardly notice. Don't be startled when you hear Whoopi Goldberg narrating *Journey to the Stars.* Seats vibrate while visitors get shot through the universe, which can be disconcerting for some, though I find it to be an appropriate jolt during my throttle through time–space continuum. Don't leave without seeing *Sonic Vision,* an alternative and rock music collaboration with MTV2, shown every Friday and Saturday evening at 7:30 p.m. and 8:30 p.m. for $15. The word "mind-blowing" is often thrown around after a screening, even by New Yorkers who pretend that nothing ever fazes them. The pumping music, 3-D

## Let's Have a Tea Party

*Alice's Tea Cup* (www.alicesteacup.com) serves up fresh scones, herbal tea served in pots, custom cakes, and treats in a quaint Alice in Wonderland themed tearoom. Though popular with little girls, it's also a favorite among women gathering for baby showers and an afternoon snack. Choose from locations at 102 West 73rd St., 156 64th St., and 220 East 81st St.

animation, digital art, and spinning visuals are enough to make you feel like you're hallucinating.

Hayden Planetarium is located at Park West at 79th Street. The museum is open daily from 10 a.m. to 5:45 p.m. and is closed Thanksgiving and Christmas Day. The Space Show is Monday through Friday every half hour from 10:30 a.m. to 4:30 p.m., on Wednesday the first show begins at 11 a.m. On weekends, 10:30 a.m. to 5 p.m. Tickets cost $16 for adults, $9 for children ages 2 to 12, seniors and students with valid ID $12. Visit www.amnh.org or call (212) 769-5200 for more information.

See where the mayor calls it a day over at *Gracie Mansion.* The sprawling estate was originally built as a country home in 1799 by Archibald Gracie to take advantage of the views over the East River. The grounds have led quite a varied life including use as a concession stand and park restrooms. Parks Commissioner Robert Moses eventually convinced city authorities to designate it as the official residence of the mayor, and in 1942, Fiorello H. La Guardia was the first tenant.

## Urban Exploring

Since its inception in 1904, the *Explorer's Club* has been hosting meetings and lectures from international adventurers, explorers, and scientists. Their Web site states the club "is an international multidisciplinary professional society dedicated to the advancement of field research and the ideal that it is vital to preserve the instinct to explore." That's a bit of an adventure to even get your head around, but explorers have flocked to see past lecturer Steve Duncan. You might know him from his tenure on the Discovery Channel as the host of "Urban Explorers." He spent about a decade climbing New York City's bridges, burrowing through empty tunnels, uncovering forgotten hospitals, and taking photographs and notes on the forgotten ruins of the city. Some of his more unique finds included exploring an empty Small Pox Hospital and the unused subway tunnel under Central Park. Beneath the bowels of Columbia University, he found remains from the Bloomingdale Insane Asylum and a cyclotron, once used by John Dunning to split an atom in 1939.

Duncan also took a look at the Red Hook Graving Docks, old rail tracks leading to the Hudson River in the '30s, and an area under Fort Totten, believed to be the longest pedestrian tunnel in New York City with "Remember the Maine" graffiti still memorializing the 1898 attack on the U.S. ship docked in a Cuban harbor.

The Explorers Club at 46 E. 70th St. (212-628-8383; www.explorers.org) discusses explorer's finds, shows photographs, and meets with other adventurers at heart with lectures open to the public a few times a month. There's also an Annual Explorers Club Film Festival held each summer. Call ahead for a schedule of public events. To find the club, take the F to Lexington and 63rd Street.

The home is also one of the oldest wood structures in Manhattan that's still standing and a member of The Historic House Trust. Gracie Mansion (212-570-4751; www.nyc.gov/html/om/html/gracie.html) is located at 180 East End Ave. and tours are offered on most Wednesdays at 10 a.m., 11 a.m., 1 p.m., and 2 p.m. Admission runs $7 for adults, $4 for seniors, and students are admitted free. Special Tea Tours are also available for groups of twenty-five to fifty people on Tuesday and Thursday. For $25, enjoy homemade tea sandwiches, teacakes, and scones.

Visitors with a penchant for aging New York mansions should visit *The Mount Vernon Hotel Museum and Garden,* operated as a hotel from 1826 until 1833. The 23-acre estate was originally a carriage house before being converted into the hotel and the grounds were once owned by Colonel William Stephens Smith and his wife, Abigail Adams Smith. History buffs will recall that the city once stopped around 14th Street, and the area that is now the Upper East Side was considered "the country." Elite New Yorkers hopped a stagecoach or took a steamboat up the river to lounge at the hotel to get away from the city. It's one of the oldest remaining buildings in Manhattan. Con Edison, one of the city's utility suppliers, purchased the building in 1905. Eventually, The Colonial Dames of America bought it in 1924. The property has since been restored and now offers tours through eight period rooms including a Lady Double Parlors, Gentlemen's Tavern Room, and Lower Hall.

The Mount Vernon Hotel Museum (212-838-6878; www.mvhm.org) can be found at 421 East 61st St. The garden is open from 11 a.m. to 4 p.m. Tuesday through Sunday and is closed during the month of August, New Year's Day, 4th of July, Thanksgiving, and Christmas day. Admission runs $8 for adults, $7 for students and seniors, and free for children 12 and under. By subway, take the N, R, 4, 5, or 6 trains to 49th Street-Lexington Avenue Station or the F train to Lexington Avenue and 63rd Street.

Continue your exploration at one of the world's largest institutions devoted to Jewish culture, *The Jewish Museum.* When it all started in 1904, the museum was housed in the library of The Jewish Theological Seminary of America until Frieda Schiff Warbug, widow of Felix, donated their family mansion on Fifth Avenue and 92nd Street to the museum in 1944. The French Gothic chateau mansion reveals the remains of Fifth Avenue's esteemed mansions peering out behind modern renovations and updates. Felix was part of a German-Jewish banking family and came to the city in 1894 and married Frieda, daughter of a partner at the banking house. The Warburgs also had a reputation for being esteemed collectors, amassing Rembrandt, Gainsborough, and a collection of prints that rivaled some of the world's finest museums. They later bequeathed 251 treasures to the nearby Metropolitan Museum of Art.

The Warburgs were trustees of the seminary and, in part, Frieda donated the mansion because of the astronomical property taxes attached to it by the 1940s. According to the book *Gilded Mansions: Grand Architecture and High Society,* the property taxes toppled as high as $665,000 a year. Even today, with Manhattan's crippling real estate prices, $665,000 could get you a sweet spot on the Upper West Side. A French Gothic chateau? Not quite, but maybe a comfortable apartment with a French bakery next door.

Today, the museum carefully displays its fine art collections in context to Jewish culture, history, and society. Of some of the popular contemporary exhibits displayed are "Too Jewish? Challenging Traditional Identities" and "Gardens and Ghettos: The Art of Jewish Life in Italy." Among its permanent exhibitions, "Culture and Continuity: The Jewish Journey" contains some 800 works of art, photos, videos, and ceremonial pieces. Aside from an impressive collection of art mirroring society all within a historical context, the gift shop itself is worth a visit. Pick up anything from sterling silver Mzuzot, Tzedakah boxes, Kiddush cups, Havdalah sets, and jewelry made by Jewish artisans. Over at the museum's Café Weissman, you can dine on contemporary kosher fare.

The Jewish Museum, located at 1109 Fifth Ave. (212-423-3200; www.the jewishmuseum.org), is open from 11 a.m. to 5:45 p.m. on Sunday through Tuesday, Thursday, and weekends. The museum is closed on Wednesday and closing hours vary on Friday; check the Web site for an updated schedule. Admission runs $12 for adults, $10 for seniors over 65, students $7.50, and children under 12 free. Visit on Saturday for free admission for all. By train, take the 4, 5, or 6 trains to 86th and Lexington.

Continue your cultural quest at *El Museo del Barrio* at 1230 Fifth Ave. and 104th Street and discover a museum dedicated to the art and culture of Puerto Rico and Latin America. Its collection includes more than 8,000 works of art, from pre-Columbian vessels to contemporary pieces. Among the hold- ings are the second-largest collection of Taino objects in the country; secular and religious pieces, including an outstanding collection of 360 *santos de palo* (carved wooden saints used for household devotions); and an exhibit docu- menting the history of print- and poster-making in Puerto Rico from the 1940s to the present.

Admission runs $9 for adults, $5 for students, and children under 12 visit free. Visiting seniors are free on Wednesday. El Museo del Barrio is closed on Monday and Tuesday, and open 11 a.m. to 6 p.m. on Wednesday through Sunday. Take the 6 train to 103rd Street; or the 2, 3 trains to 110th and Lenox Avenue. Call (212) 831-7272 or visit www.elmuseo.org for more information.

If you're drowning in a sea of museums, history, and modern buildings, and just want to "find" the city already, head to the **Museum of the City of New York.** Here you can wrap your head around the past, present, and future of the city. Wind through the exhibits of fashion and costumes, maps, dioramas, prints, sculptures, and artifacts through New York's history. You can learn more about New York as a Dutch colony, to the foothold of the British and George Washington securing his presidency, to modern-day era. Look for the John D. Rockefeller exhibit showcasing his master bedroom, and a walk through Broadway theater's history. If your kids are tired of the museum scene, take them to the *"New York Toy Stories"* exhibit stuffed with dolls, toys, games, puzzles, and trinkets of the city's children, including the Stettheimer Doll House of the 1920s complete with a tiny art gallery.

The Museum of the City of New York (212-534-1672; www.mcny.org) is located at 1220 Fifth Ave. at 103rd Street, and is open Tuesday through Sunday from 10 a.m. to 5 p.m. and open on major Monday holidays. The museum is closed Thanksgiving, Christmas, and New Year's Day. There is a suggested admission of $10 for adults, $6 for seniors and students, and children 12 and under are free. Families with a max of two adults pay $20. By subway, take the 6 to 103rd Street, or the 2 or 3 trains to 110th Street and Central Park North.

If you started your journey down by Battery Park, made your way up the Esplanade, well past the Frying Pan and Intrepid Sea, Air & Space Museum and beyond, you would have eventually ended up at **Riverside Park** (www .nycgovparks.org/sub_your_park/vt_riverside_park/vt_riverside_park.html) along the Hudson at 72nd. But unless you have the time and energy for a marathon adventure, take the train up. The park stretches all the way to 158th Street with views well worth the journey along the wooded shores of the Hudson.

## An Act of God

In 1870 the American actor Joseph Jefferson went to a church near the spot where the Empire State Building now stands to arrange for a friend's burial service. Upon learning that the deceased was an actor, the rector suggested that Jefferson make arrangements at a church around the corner. Jefferson is said to have replied, "Thank God for the little church around the corner," and that's how the **Church of the Transfiguration** at 1 East Twenty-ninth St. got its nicknames, "Little Church Around the Corner" and the "Actors' Church." Over the years grateful thespians, including Sarah Bernhardt, have worshiped here, and there are memorial windows to actors such as John Drew, Edwin Booth, and Richard Mansfield.

From your spot marveling over the views in Riverside Park and wondering how much real estate costs around these parts, look for the curious collection of boats dotting the *79th Street Boat Basin.* A handful of lucky Manhattanites live right on these teetering houseboats year-round. In 2008, the *New York Times* ran a feature about renting boat space in the basin for a mere $490. It's true that some might say these house boaters are nothing more than squatters on public ground. But I enjoy their mystery and intimacy as they quietly bob along the surface of the Hudson. The city stopped issuing permits to dock full-time in 1994, and only recently allowed a limited number of new permits to be issued annually.

Nearby in the neighborhood of Morningside Heights, pay your respects at *Grant's Tomb.* While tourists and locals may know it as the resting place of General Ulysses S. Grant, they may not realize it is the largest tomb in North America. From the top of the hill where the tomb rests, look down for daz-zling views of the Hudson River. The park also puts on birthday celebrations for the nearly 200-year-old general, night tours, and Memorial Day events. To reach the tomb (www.nps.gov/gegr/index.htm), take the 1 train to 116th Street-Columbia University.

As you venture deeper into Northern Manhattan, you'll see why it's one of my favorite places in the city to explore. Rocky outcroppings, elevated tree lines, and rolling landscape provide a tranquil oasis from the urban jungle. Make your way to the Hamilton Heights neighborhood to find *Riverbank State Park,* the city's only state park. With a reputation as "the only park of its kind in the Western Hemisphere," the park was influenced by urban rooftop designs in Japan across 28 acres. The landscape takes a multi-level approach, giving it a vertical feel as you venture 69 feet above the Hudson River. From the promenade, gaze down at the Hudson, across to the Palisade Mountains, and over at the George Washington Bridge. (Look toward the legs of the Manhattan side of the bridge to see if you can spot the Little Red Lighthouse, mentioned in this book.)

If the breathtaking views aren't enough for you, an ice skating rink, per-forming arts center, playgrounds, an Olympic-sized swimming pool, gymnasium, tennis, roller skating, and picnic tables abound. The park is also dedicated to bringing programs to locals, featuring nearly 400 programs throughout the year including free jazz concerts, children's performing arts "popsicle series," Pilates and salsa lessons, and summer theater festivals. Visitors on a budget can go roller skating for as little as $1.50 with a $6 a day rental, hit the pool for $2, and use a fitness room for $10 per day. Or just stroll throughout the grounds for free.

Make your way to the *Totally Kids Carousel,* created by artist Milo Mottola and neighborhood kids from the area. Unlike the historic carousels at Central Park and in DUMBO, Riverbank's houses a collection of brightly colored, mismatched animals. An alligator, bat, frog, lizard, lobster, peacock, a two-headed octopus, snail, T. Rex, and whale are just some of the creatures guests can hop a ride on. The neighborhood kids drew pictures of the animals and Mottolla brought their creations to life in 1997. But instead of interpreting their drawings and refining the dimensions into more traditional works of art, Mottolla left them in true "kid-form" with bright colors, quirky proportions, and raw detailing. Weather permitting, the carousel is usually open from 1 to 6 p.m. every day except Wednesday.

Riverbank State Park is open from 6 a.m. to 11 p.m. year-round with ice skating from November to January (check the Web site for seasonal hours) and roller skating through the rest of the year. To get to Riverbank State Park (679 Riverside Dr.; nysparks.state.ny.us/parks/93/details.aspx), take the 1 train to 145th Street and walk west toward Broadway. Call (212) 694-3600 for more information.

The only operating cemetery left in Manhattan lies along a swatch near the picturesque Riverside Drive. *Trinity Cemetery and Mausoleum* sprawls across two plots dissected by Broadway. Unlike many of the former potter's cemeteries earmarked for the city's poor, Trinity Cemetery was reserved for Manhattan's elite. John James Audubon, the artist and naturalist, rests on the eastern side of the cemetery marked by a memorial topped by a Celtic cross. Currently, only a handful of available above-ground graves remain, reportedly reserved for "special citizens." For all the not so special citizens on a budget, spots in the mausoleum are reportedly up for grabs.

If you've already explored some of the historic spots of Northern Manhattan listed in this book, you'll guess right that the Revolutionary War is entangled in the roots of this cemetery. The grounds were home to the Battle of Harlem Heights in 1776. Just as impressive as the marble and granite crypts, the grounds are also full of 100-year-old oak and elms trees. During Christmas, a candlelight ceremony is held at the gravesite of Clement Clarke Moore, author of the poem *A Visit From St. Nicholas,* better known as *'Twas the Night Before Christmas.* Take a stroll through the plots and take in the family crypts including actor Jerry Orbach.

The Trinity Cemetery and Mausoleum (212-368-1600; www.trinitywall street.org/congregation/cemetery) is located at 770 Riverside Dr. By subway, take the 1 to 157th Street, or the C to 155th Street.

Manhattan's only lighthouse can be found in the shadow of the George Washington Bridge on *Jeffrey's Hook* (Fort Washington Park at 178th Street; 212-304-2365; www.nycgovparks.org/sub_about/parks_divisions/ historic_houses/hh_little_red_light.html). Built in 1880 on Sandy Hook, New

Jersey, the 40-foot-tall Little Red Lighthouse was dismantled in 1917 and reconstructed in 1921 on Jeffrey's Hook, where it continued to operate until 1947. The little beacon was made famous by the 1942 children's book *The Little Red Lighthouse and the Great Gray Bridge* by Hildegarde Swift and Lynd Ward. In the book, the lighthouse is content and happy until a giant bridge is built over it, but he eventually learns he still has an important job to do.

With such a cute, heartwarming story to share, it's no wonder that in 1951 there was a panicked, public outcry when a proposal threatened the removal of the lighthouse. Many of its supporters were children and parents who cherished the book. Supporters collected money and started campaigning to keep the lighthouse standing. The city listened and the preservation of the lighthouse was transferred to the City of New York Parks and Recreation. Today, there is an annual festival held at the lighthouse every September and includes celebrity readings of *The Little Red Lighthouse* classic. Past readers have included Isabella Rossellini, Dee Dee Conn, and James Earl Jones. Some say the book itself saved the lighthouse.

Today Jeffrey's Hook Lighthouse, with its forty-eight brightly painted cast-iron plates, is a part of the Historic House Trust of New York City. During special events, visitors can climb the spiral staircase to an observation deck that looks out across the river at the Palisades. Exhibition panels at the base provide information about the river. The Little Red Lighthouse is open for public tours.

Do a little planning before you head out to find it, it's easy to miss. Even though I knew this little guy was somewhere underneath the George Washington Bridge, I never noticed that its little red silhouette resting next to George's leg was actually visible from the Henry Hudson Parkway. By subway, take the A train to 181st Street and take the steps down to the footpath and footbridge. Make your way down to Fort Washington Park and head south until you reach the lighthouse waiting to greet you against its rocky shore.

Continue heading North on the Hudson and visit **Fort Tyron Park** (www.nycgovparks.org/parks/forttryonpark) encompassing Riverside Drive to Broadway and West 192nd to Dyckman Streets. The park was built in 1935 by Frederick Law Olmsted Jr. If his surname sounds familiar, it might be because Olmsted's father was Central Park's famed architect. Aside from its recreational grounds, dog run, gazebo, and playgrounds, the park also features a haven for art. Its northern grounds hold the area often referred to as "The Cloisters" by locals. The Cloisters is a branch of the Metropolitan Museum of Art housed inside an authentic, reconstructed medieval monastery holding nearly 5,000 medieval works on display.

The Cloisters is one of the most vertical parks I've ever explored. You can hardly go ten feet without stumbling across a winding staircase, rocky walls, tunnels, and multiple levels with vantage points of the Hudson. Head down to Heathers Gardens and enjoy the blooms. Hungry? The park's *New Leaf Restaurant and Bar,* founded by Bette Midler's New York Restoration Project, features a handful of works of art in its own right. Guests savor spicy salmon tartare, crisp duck steak, and sliced leg of lamb before mouth-watering crème brulee, fresh sorbets, and brioche bread pudding. Order up, proceeds go to the restoration and preservation of Fort Tyron Park. Housed in a 1930s stone structure, the restaurant also hosts Friday night jazz performances.

The restaurant is located at 1 Margaret Corbin Dr. (212-333-2552; www .nyrp.org) and is closed on Monday. Dine Tuesday through Friday from noon to 3:30 p.m. and again at 6 to 10 p.m. On Saturday, the New Leaf is open 11 a.m. to 3:30 p.m. and 6 to 10 p.m. On Sunday, it is open 11 a.m. to 3:30 p.m. and 5:30 to 9:30 p.m. Take the A train to 190th Street.

Want to see some of the oldest culture you'll find in the city? Northern Manhattan's 196-acre *Inwood Hill Park* reflects the city's earliest caves, valleys, and ridges brushing up against a dense forest. It also houses Manhattan's last natural salt marsh. Stop by the Nature Center for a map and information on the history of the park. Learn about Shorakkopoch, a Lenape Indian village that Peter Stuyvesant bought for 60 guilders, a mere $35 in today's dollars. (You probably dropped that much by lunchtime during your visit.) You can still see the rock marking the site of the village. Take time to read the plaque unfolding the story of a 220-year-old tulip poplar, native to Manhattan that was the last living link to the Reckgawawang inhabitants of Manhattan.

Hike the trails the Native Americans used as footpaths and rows and pass Indian Rock Shelters and look for bald eagles; the city is trying to reintroduce them to the park. Although the park still boasts a beautiful forest, the park once held a public library and a charity house for women during the 1800s. Along with wooded nature trails, baseball fields, basketball courts, dog courts, and playgrounds can be found in the park.

It is strongly advisable to hike with a partner and a map from the Nature Center, as the park's trail can be secluded. Inwood Hill Park is located at 218th Street and Indian Road (212-304-2365; www.nycgovparks.org/parks/inwood hillpark). By subway, take the IND A train to 200th and Dyckman Street.

Did you know that beyond Manhattan's towering apartment complexes and brownstones lies a farmhouse? The *Dyckman Farmhouse Museum* represents a link to Manhattan's rural farming lifestyle, swallowed by an urban city. The museum is the actual location where the house has stood since 1784. The Dyckman sisters bought the home in 1915 with hopes of restoring and preserving the home and opened it to the public the following year. The museum carefully depicts farm and city culture with various details from 1815 to 1820, and 1915 to 1916, when Manhattan began transforming and leaving behind its rural roots.

The museum is a representation of Manhattan's past, rather than an exact exhibit of what the house itself once was. But the house does give clues to its past, including a cider mill in the farmyard that indicated apple trees once stood. Historians suspect cherry trees and fruit orchards once thrived in the area. Nearly a century ago, amateur archaeologists scoured Manhattan's northern tip to search for the city's rural history. Many of those thousand of objects they uncovered were later donated to the museum. Old cannon balls, bayonet points, and Revolutionary War memorabilia are now on display. The museum is working to research and organize its vast collection to exhibit. I take for granted how metropolitan and developed the city is, I wonder what would happen if I started my own excavation in the middle of a nearby park.

The Dyckman Farmhouse can be found at 4881 Broadway at 204th Street and is open Wednesday through Saturday from 11 a.m. to 4 p.m. and Sunday from noon to 4 p.m. The farmhouse is closed Easter Sunday, 4th of July, Thanksgiving and Christmas Day, December 26 and 31, and New Year's Day. Admission runs $1 for adults and free for children under 10. Take the A, 1, or 9 to 207th Street. Check www.dyckmanfarmhouse.org or call (212) 304-9422 for more information on events and updated tours.

# Tours

Acclimate yourself with the city by foot or a tour to get a sampling of everything it has to offer. If you're like me, you'll want to somehow combine the act of eating as much food as possible with your touring experience, and New York has plenty of stops for flavorful consumption. The *Lower East Side Artisan Food Highlights Tour* focuses on the old and new restaurants and dishes of the thriving Lower East Side. See popular classics including Russ & Daughter's, Kossar's Bialys, and Yonah Schimmel knishes. Then get a taste of exotic donuts, fresh dill pickles, and creamy mission fig and chocolate chili ice cream. (Just hopefully not all during one sitting.) Call (212) 209-3370 for more information.

If you have a more refined palate and are looking for something soothing, enjoy a day in the city while learning and tasting tea on a *Tea with Friends Tour.* Choose from the Japanese Tea Tour, the World in a Teacup French and English Tea Tour, and Asian Tradition Tour. Call (866) 616-1154 for more information.

***The Brooklyn Food Tour,*** the ***Best Of Brooklyn Multicultural Ethnic Neighborhood Food Tasting and Culture Tour*** (that's a mouthful) covers everything from Cuban sandwiches to fine chocolates while eating your way through Old Williamsburg, DUMBO, and Sunset Park. Call (800) 979-3370. (For more on DUMBO, see the Brooklyn chapter.)

Though not on the food trail, the ***Flatiron Building Walking Tour*** features one of my favorite pieces of architecture in the city. Also known as the Fuller Building, it's 285 feet high. Unfortunately, the building is just full of offices and cubicles, so there's really nothing to tour on the inside. The outside, however, is worth the trip. The Flatiron and 23rd Street Partnership sponsors free New York City walking tours of the historic Flatiron district every Sunday at 11 a.m. Call (212) 741-2323 for more information.

Just south of the Flatiron Building, Union Square Park houses one of my favorite farmers' markets in the city. I used to work in the area and would pick out a piece of fruit from the crowd of vendors on my way from the subway to work. The park offers a 90-minute free ***Union Square Walking Tour*** every Saturday at 2 p.m. called "Union Square: Crossroads of New York." Visitors get an overview of the neighborhood and a lesson in its history, people, architecture, and politics. Call (212) 517-1826 for more information.

I generally skirt around Times Square at all costs. Missing the gritty history of Times Square past with a ***Times Square Walking Tour***? Wishing you were there pre-Disney? Enjoy everything today's Times Square has to offer, but with all the gossip of its sordid past. Maybe you'll get to see the Naked Cowboy performing on your free New York City tour. Meet at the Times Square Visitors Center at 1560 Broadway, between 46th and 47th Streets Friday at noon.

Rich in history, tradition, music, and food, Harlem is enjoying an ongoing renaissance, reflected in strong property prices and the influx of new businesses. Companies have plenty of competition and offer specialized tours of the area. The menu of Harlem Spirituals tours include "Harlem

## City Pass

First-time visitors looking for some of the city's most popular attractions on a budget should pick-up a *CityPass*, a $140 value priced at $79 (ages 6 to 17, $59). The pass includes admission to the American Museum of Natural History and Rose Center, the Museum of Modern Art, the Empire State Building Observatory, the Guggenheim Museum, the Metropolitan Museum of Art, and The Cloisters, and a choice of Circle Line Sightseeing Cruises or Statue of Liberty and Ellis Island. For more information call (888) 330-5008 or visit www.citypass.com.

Gospel on Sunday," complete with a church service, a soul-food brunch, and "Soul Food and Jazz." Multilingual tours are available; reservations are required. **Harlem Spirituals,** 690 8th Ave. (between 43rd and 44th Streets). Call (800) 660-2166 or (212) 391-0900 or visit www.harlemspirituals.com for more information.

**The Studio Museum** (144 West 125th St.; 212-864-4500; www.studio museum.org) in Harlem was founded in 1967 as a working and exhibition space for African-American artists. Today, the country's first accredited African-American fine arts museum houses an extensive collection of nineteenth- and twentieth-century African-American art, twentieth-century Caribbean and African art, and traditional African art and artifacts. But this 60,000-square-foot building is more than a museum. It's a center for interpreting its contents to both children and adults. In addition to an artists-in-residence program and an outreach program for Harlem's public schools, the museum hosts numerous workshops, arts and humanities programs, and special exhibits throughout the year.

The Studio Museum in Harlem is open Wednesday to Friday noon to 6 p.m., Saturday from 10 a.m. to 6 p.m., and Sunday noon to 6 p.m. The museum is closed on Monday, Tuesday, and major holidays. Suggested donation is $7 for adults, $3 for students and seniors, free for those under 12. Take the 2, 3, A, B, C, D, 4, 5, or 6 trains to 125th Street in Harlem.

## eggcream

There are no eggs or cream in the egg cream, though some sources say that the original fountain drink, still beloved by New Yorkers, used syrup made with eggs and mixed with cream to give a rich taste. The egg cream as we know it today is a tasty concoction of milk, chocolate syrup, and seltzer—and costs more than the nickel originally charged.

Although the **Apollo Theater** at 253 West 125th St. is well on the beaten path, you can stop in for a behind-the-scenes tour, explore the neighborhood, or see a show. The theater continues to stand as a historic venue featuring open houses, lectures, and featured entertainment. In 2009 *Dreamgirls* opened at the Apollo before embarking on a nationwide tour. Before taking in a performance, enjoy dinner at **Revival** (2367 8th Ave., 212-222-8338; www.harlem revival.com) for divine cornbread mushroom appetizers, Caribbean style lamb patties, gospel pasta soup, cider brined spare ribs, and red snapper linguini. The restaurant frequently offers discounts to patrons with tickets to same night performances at the Apollo.

Tour the Apollo Theater (212-531-5300; www.apollotheater.org) on Monday, Tuesday, Thursday and Friday at 11 a.m., 1 p.m., and 3 p.m. Wednesday tours are only available at 11 a.m., and weekend tours start at 11 a.m. and 1 p.m. General admission runs $16 a person on weekdays and $18 on weekends.

While in Harlem, head over to **The Cathedral Church of Saint John the Divine** for a heavenly ascent up 124 feet of spiral stone staircase. Under construction since 1892 (and counting), it is the largest Gothic cathedral in the world and could blanket the Statue of Liberty with room to spare. Despite its Gothic influence, the cathedral also features ornate Romanesque detailing. The cathedral was meticulously planned and built around the mystery of the number 7. For example, the buttresses are 124 feet tall (1+2+4=7).

The cathedral's Vertical Tour features an inside look at the ongoing restoration process, stained glass windows featuring Thomas Aquinas, intricate stonework, hidden passageways, and views of Morningside Heights from its rooftop. I wish I had known about this tour during my first decade in New York, where I would have taken anyone willing, except my claustrophobic Mom. This tour is not for anyone with space anxieties or timid in dark places— flashlights are handed out at the onset of the journey up. After your descent from the roof, take a stroll through the lush Biblical Gardens for a breath of fresh air. Visitors might be startled to find peacocks wandering through the cherry trees, and a Peace Fountain on 13 acres of garden.

Take a moment to inspect the breathtaking stained glass enveloping the cathedral. At first glance, you might marvel at the artisanship and fine crafting and liken it to what you saw on your trip to Rome last year. Look closer. See anything out of place? Your eyes might stumble across George Washington and Abraham Lincoln in one panel, Benjamin Franklin in another, and even a sinking *Titanic* in yet another. It gets stranger. Wait until you see the guys bowling in another ornate stained glass panel.

The church also offers Spotlight on Geometry and Numerology, the Middle Ages, and Symbolism tours among others. The Cathedral Church of Saint John the Divine (212-932-7347; www.stjohndivine.org) is located at 1047 Amsterdam Ave. Advance reservations are required and the tour tops out at ten people. Admission runs $15 for adults and $10 for students and seniors. Check the Web site for current times, tours, and prices. By train, take the 1 or 9 trains to 110th Street-Cathedral Station.

Discover Manhattan's oldest house tucked away in historic Harlem. **The Morris-Jumel Mansion** dates back to 1765, when British Colonel Roger Morris and his American wife, Mary Philips, built their summer home high on a hill. The area was formerly known as Mount Morris and covered over 130 acres across Harlem to the Hudson River. Morris was eventually forced back to England during the Revolutionary War.

The estate became a strategic military point and eventually the headquarters of George Washington in 1776. His troops successfully forced a British retreat during the Battle of Harlem Heights. Over the years, the mansion became an inn before it was restored in 1810 by French immigrants Stephen Jumel and his wife, Eliza. Stephen eventually died and Eliza, one of the wealthiest women in New York during her time, married Vice President Aaron Burr. After they split two years later, Eliza kept the home until her death.

The 8,500-square-foot Palladian style mansion features classical columns, a balcony, original hearth, bee-hive oven, and a two-story octagonal drawing room in the rear of the house. Visitors can peruse the parlor where Eliza and Aaron Burr married.

The mansion (212-923-8008; www.morrisjumel.org) is located at 65 Jumel Terrace and is open at 10 a.m. on Wednesday through Sunday and by appointment only on Monday and Tuesday. The museum is closed on New Year's Day, Memorial Day, Independence Day, Labor Day, Thanksgiving Day, and Christmas Day. Admission runs $5 adults, $4 seniors and students, and free for children 12 and under with a paying adult. By subway, take the C train to 163rd Street.

# Places to Eat in Manhattan

Use this list as a reference for places to try when you're drowning in an endless sea of restaurant options, but don't use it to replace the chance to explore a culinary adventure. Although the city can make your head spin with restaurants sitting on top of restaurants to choose from, the upside is bad meals are hard to come by in a city where competition is cut-throat. Check www .menupages.com for menus, directions, and reviews to just about any eatery in the city.

**Adour Alain Ducasse**
2 E. 55th St.
(212) 710-2277
www.adour-stregis.com

**Alto**
11 E. 53rd St.
(212) 308-1099
www.altorestaurant.com

**Anthos**
36 W 52nd St.
(212) 582-6900
www.anthosnyc.com

**Aquagrill**
210 Spring St.
(212) 274-0505
www.aquagrill.com

**Aquavit**
65 E. 55th St.
(212) 307-7311
ww.aquavit.org

**B Flat**
277 Church St.
(212) 219-2970
www.bflat.info

**Bar Boulud**
1900 Broadway
(212) 595-0303
www.danielnyc.com

**Bar Stuzzichini**
928 Broadway
(212) 780-5100
www.barstuzzichini.com

**Becco**
355 West 46th St.
(212) 397-7597
www.becconyc.com

**Blue Ribbon Sushi Bar & Grill**
308 W 58th St.
(212) 397-0404
www.blueribbonrestaurants.com

**Caracas**
91 E 7th St.
(212) 228-5062
www.caracasarepabar.com

**Carnegie Deli**
854 7th Ave.
(212) 757-2245
www.carnegiedeli.com

**Cascina**
647 9th Ave.
(212) 245-4422
www.cascina.com

**Centrico**
211 West Broadway
(212) 431-0700
www.myriadrestaurant group.com

**Chez Josephine**
414 West 42nd St.
(212) 594-1925
www.chezjosephine.com

**Dell'anima**
38 8th Ave.
(212) 366-6633
www.dellanima.com

**Dovetail**
103 W. 77th St.
(212) 362-3800
www.dovetailnyc.com

**El Quinto Pino**
401 W. 24th St.
(212) 206-6900
www.elquintopinonyc.com

**Gotham Bar and Grill**
12 East 12th St.
(212) 620-4020
www.gothambarandgrill.com

**Graffiti Food and Wine Bar**
224 E. 10th St.
(212) 464-7743
www.graffitinyc.com

**Hill Country**
30 W. 26th St.
(212) 255-4544
www.hillcountryny.com

**Insieme**
777 7th Ave.
(212) 582-1310
www.restaurantinsieme.com

**Kingswood**
122 W. 10th St.
(212) 645-0018
www.kingswoodnyc.com

**L'Ecole**
French Culinary Institute
462 Broadway
(212) 219-3300
www.frenchculinary.com

**Le Pain Quotidien**
Many city locations;
check Web site
www.painquotidien.com

**Milk and Honey**
134 Eldridge St.
(212) 625-3397
www.mlkhny.com

**Momofuku Ko**
163 1st Ave.
(212) 500-0831
www.momofuku.com

**Montebello**
120 East 56th St.
(212) 753-1447
www.montebellonyc.com

**The New French**
522 Hudson St.
(212) 807-7357

**Nobu**
40 W 57th St.
(212) 757-3000
www.noburestaurants.com

**Payard Bistro**
1032 Lexington Ave.
(212) 717-5252
www.payard.com

**Porchetta**
110 E. 7th St.
(212) 777-2151
www.porchettanyc.com

**Resto**
111 E. 29th St.
(212) 685-5585
www.restonyc.com

**Shun Lee Palace**
155 East 55th St.
(212) 371-8844
www.shunleepalace.com

**Sunita**
106 Norfolk St.
(212) 253-8860
www.sunitabar.com

**Sylvia's**
328 Lenox Ave.
Harlem
(212) 996-0660
www.sylviasoulfood.com

**Terrace in the Sky**
400 West 119th St.
(212) 666-9490
www.terraceinthesky.com

**Turkish Cuisine**
631 9th Ave.
(212) 397-9650

**Yerba Buena**
23 Ave. A
(212) 529-2919
www.ybnyc.com

# THE BRONX

→

Keep reaching north to arrive at the only borough of the city of New York *not* located on an island: the Bronx. It was named for Swedish commercial sea captain Jonas Bronck, who, in 1639, became the first European settler to establish residency in this area.

With a population of nearly 1.4 million, the Bronx claims a number of famous people who have lived here: performers Anne Bancroft, Tony Curtis, Robert Klein, Hal Linden, Penny and Gary Marshall, Rita Moreno, Chazz Palminteri, Roberta Peters, Regis Philbin, Jennifer Lopez, and Carl Reiner; athletes Lou Gehrig and Jake La Motta; authors E. L. Doctorow, Theodore Dreiser, Edgar Allan Poe, Mark Twain, and Herman Wouk; statesmen John Adams, John F. Kennedy, and Colin Powell; designers Calvin Klein and Ralph Lauren; and the conductor Arturo Toscanini.

The Bronx's golden age in the 1920s saw the building of the "El," an elevated subway line, Yankee Stadium, the mile-long Grand Concourse (which many likened to the Champs Elysées in Paris), and a population boom.

Artifacts of that history—and even earlier dating back to the eighteenth century—can be found in the *Museum of History.* The museum is located in a fieldstone house built in

1758 called the **Valentine-Varian House,** which looks as if it would be more at home on a farm in Pennsylvania than in the borough of endless row houses and sky-high apartment buildings.

The Valentine-Varian House (3266 Bainbridge Ave. at 208th Street; 718-881-8900) is open Saturday from 10 a.m. to 4 p.m., Sunday from 1 to 5 p.m., and weekdays by appointment. Admission runs $5 for adults and $3 for children, students, and seniors. The County Historical Society, which administers the museum and the Poe Cottage, offers tours of the house, as well as a lecture series. Call for a schedule or visit www.historicalsociety.org.

An important chapter in history and in the history of literature relates to a thirty-seven-year-old poet, short-story writer, and critic named Edgar Allan Poe. In 1846 Poe rented a small wooden cottage, now known as the Poe Cottage, in Poe Park, East Kingsbridge Road and the Grand Concourse, not far from the campus of Fordham University. (In Poe's day the school was known as St. John's College.) Poe's wife was in fragile health and it was thought that the country was a more salubrious environment than the couple's former home, New York City. But Virginia Clemm Poe, who was also the writer's cousin, died of tuberculosis early in 1847, leaving Poe in the state of despondency reflected in his poem, "Annabel Lee," and other melancholy verse.

Poe maintained his residence even after his wife's death, drinking like a fish and trying to keep up with his bills by delivering an occasional lecture. While returning from one of his lecture trips, he died in Baltimore in 1849.

The world often cares for the homes and artifacts of its dead poets more than it does its living ones, much like Edgar Allan Poe. Though the rapidly growing city nearly swallowed the Poe Cottage during the latter half of the nineteenth century, the city got wise in 1902 and dedicated a park in his honor across the street from the house. The house was moved to the park eleven years later and opened as a museum in 1917.

You can find **The Edgar Allan Poe Cottage** (718-881-8900; www.nyc govparks.org/sub_about/parks_divisions/historic_houses/hh_edgar_allan_poe .html) at Grand Concourse and East Kingsbridge Road open Saturday 10 a.m. to 4 p.m. and Sunday 1 to 5 p.m. throughout the year. Admission is $5 for adults and $3 for students, seniors, and children. By subway, take the D or 4 trains to Kingsbridge Road.

Despite the city's rapid growth, not all of the land was consumed by developers, 24 percent of its 42 square miles still features green space, a greater percentage than any other urban area in the country.

Discover some of the borough's 6,000 acres of green space at the **New York Botanical and Zoological Gardens, Van Cortlandt Park,** and

*Pelham Bay Park.* But a visit to the Bronx should also include a stop at *Wave Hill,* a 28-acre preserve in the Riverdale neighborhood at its northwest corner. Wave Hill is not a wilderness, but a section of the borough that remained in its natural state until the middle of the last century, when it was first acquired as a country estate. Today, Wave Hill is the only one of the great Hudson River estates within the city limits preserved for public use.

In 1836 New York lawyer William Morris bought fifteen acres of river-bank real estate and built Wave Hill House, one of the two mansions that today grace the property, as a summer retreat. Thirty years later the Morris tract was acquired by publisher William Appleton, who remodeled the house and began developing the gardens and conservatories for which the property would become famous. Appleton was known to bring around natural scientists to brag about his digs. Among them was Thomas Henry Huxley, who was so astounded, he looked across the water at the Palisades and proclaimed it one of the world's greatest natural wonders. Financier George Perkins bought the estate in 1893 and increased its size to eighty acres, with a scattering of six fine houses, including Wave Hill and Glyndor, which had been built by Oliver Har-riman. Burned in 1927, Glyndor was rebuilt by Perkins' widow, and Glyndor II, as it is known, is still a part of the Wave Hill property.

Today, the attractions of Wave Hill include art exhibits, concert series, outdoor dance performances, and special events. But its shining star is still the landscape, with some grounds manicured and some relatively untouched. There are 350 varieties of trees and shrubs and wild and cultivated flowers lining the gardens, greenhouses, and pathways of the estate. A ten-acre section of woods has been restored as a native forest environment, complete with elderberries, witch hazel, and native grasses. I'm a personal fan of the wooded nature trail around the grounds leading to a hidden gazebo and views of the Bronx you never knew existed.

Wave Hill, 249th Street and Independence Avenue (718-549-3200, www .wavehill.org) is open Tuesday through Sunday, mid-April through mid-October, 9 a.m. to 5:30 p.m., and 9 a.m. to 4:30 p.m. from mid-October through mid-April. The greenhouses are open from 10 a.m. to noon and 2 to 4 p.m.; closed Christmas and New Year's Day. Admission is free all day Tuesday, until noon Saturday, and during December,

## nyisland

Look at a map and you'll see that Manhattan and Staten Island are islands; while Queens and Brooklyn are on the western tip of Long Island. That means that of New York City's five boroughs, only the Bronx is part of the mainland. However, there is an island that's part of the borough: City Island. In 1898 the five boroughs were incorporated into a single entity, known as Greater New York.

January, and February. Other days, admission is $4 for adults, $2 for seniors and students, and free for children 6 and under. Tours are given each Sunday at 2:15 p.m. The cafe is open for lunch and snacks.

While Manhattan's museums boast grandiose collections of artists from days gone by, the permanent collection at the *Museum of the Arts* focuses on the work of contemporary artists of African, Asian, and Latin American descent. It has presented hundreds of critically acclaimed exhibitions featuring works by culturally diverse and under-recognized artists.

The Museum of the Arts, 1040 Grand Concourse (at 165th Street; 718-681-6000; www.museum.org), is open on Thursday from 11 a.m. to 6 p.m., Friday 11 a.m. to 8 p.m., and Saturday and Sunday from 1 to 6 p.m., and is closed Thanksgiving, Christmas, and New Year's Day. Admission runs $5 for adults, $3 for students and seniors, free for children under 12 years old, and free to the public on Friday. To reach the museum, take the D or B trains to 167th Street-Grand Concourse or the 4 train to 161st Street.

Even locals I know have never heard of the Little Italy in the Bronx on Belmont and Arthur Avenues. Discover colorful and delicious food in markets overflowing with fruits, vegetables, salamis and sausages, homemade mozzarella, a rainbow of olives, luscious pastries, and breads.

A personal favorite: the mouthwatering sandwiches of mozzarella and prosciutto at *Mike's Deli* at 2344 Arthur Ave. (718-295-5033; www.arthuravenue .com). Visit old-world Italy at *La Casa del Caffe* at 1036 Morris Park Ave. (718-931-7816) and sit at the outdoor tables for a cup of cappuccino or a gelato. For crisp, brick oven pizzas, try *Patricia's* at 1080 Morris Park Ave., and top off your day with a sfogliatelle, fruit tart, or Italian ice at *Enrico's Pastry Shop* at 1057 Morris Park Ave.

The campus at Bronx Community College was once a part of New York University and its chancellor, during 1901, decided a hall of fame should be erected. Hence the *Hall of Fame for Great Americans* was born to pay homage to prominent Americans who helped shape our society. A 630-foot open-air colonnade features bronze portrait busts. Built by renowned architect Stanford White, the museum is located within a New York City landmark that is also on the National Register of Historic Places. Such notable Americans as Presidents John Adams, John Quincy Adams, naturalist Louis Agassiz, artist John James Audubon, and nurse Clara Barton are waiting to greet visitors. Currently, there are ninety-eight great Americans on display arranged by authors, scientists, teachers, soldiers, jurists, and statesmen. Take a moment to read the plaques accompanying the busts to see what the person did and why he or she is famous. Perhaps just as impressive as the idea of honoring great Americans is the view of the Palisades from the open-air colonnade the hall sits in.

The Hall of Fame for Great Americans (718-289-5161) is open daily from 10 a.m. to 5 p.m., admission is free. By subway, take the 4 train to Burnside Avenue and Jerome Avenue. You can see an online video of the busts on display at www.bcc.cuny.edu/halloffame.

The Bronx is, unfortunately, often overlooked for its variety of stunning waterfront, sprawling parks, and green space. Nestled in Pellham Bay Park in the Bronx, *Orchard Beach* (www.nycgovparks.org/parks/orchardbeach) is the Bronx's only beach. It was originally dubbed the "Riviera of New York" and includes a promenade with boutiques and recreational areas. Popular year-round, spend a day cooling off, walking, or playing a spirited game of basketball with the locals. I have a feeling Bronx residents prefer the rest of the city overlooking their green space and keeping the secret to themselves.

If you think Manhattan holds the title of largest park in the city with Central Park, you're wrong. The Bronx wins the nod with *Pelham Bay Park* (www.nycgovparks.org/sub_your_park/vt_pelham_bay_park/vt_pelham_bay_park.html). The green expanse of Pelham Bay features over 2,700 acres with a Thomas Pell Wildlife Sanctuary home to salt marshes and egrets, herons, and red-winged blackbirds. Visitors can also get off the well-worn path littered with picnics, weekend birthday parties, and joggers by heading to the park's Hunter Island. The island was named for John Hunter whose mansion sat on the highest point on the island and who was known to rub elbows with some of the country's elite. In 1839, President Martin Van Buren visited the grounds to see Hunter's art collection.

The sign "Welcome to City Island, Seaport of the Bronx" welcomes visitors and locals home to *City Island* (www.cityisland.com). Although there are not many attractions and stops counted by guide books in the tiny neighborhood, I've fallen in love with its charm. The island is about 1½ miles long by ½ mile wide and resembles a quaint New England fishing town. The island is peppered with lobster and seafood restaurants, pubs, and yacht clubs. Despite the abundance of fresh seafood for sale, none of it actually comes from City Island; it's all imported due to polluted waters and mandates from the New York State Department of Health.

Nestled on the extreme west end of the Long Island Sound, City Island was once part of Westchester and became a part of the Bronx and is connected to the rest of the borough by the City Island Bridge. Residents drive or take an express bus into Manhattan, only available a few times a day, or take the 6 train into the Bronx before switching to the BX29 to cross the bridge.

Over the years, I wondered why green parrots, or monk parakeets, frequented Manhattan. I learned they were originally imported from South

## Not for the Faint of Hart

On the northeast shoreline of City Island, look for **Hart Island** (www.correctionhistory
.org/html/chronicl/nycdoc/html/hart.html), a nearly inaccessible island, and practically
forgotten by most locals. Dubbed "The Island of the Dead," it was once a war camp,
sanitarium, and potter's field and is currently the largest tax funded cemetery in the
world. Prisoners from Riker's Island performed mass burials on the island. Abandoned buildings, prison houses, and grave sites are all that remain. Michael Douglas
filmed there during *Don't Say a Word,* as well as the cast and crew of (appropriately
named) *Island of the Dead.* The few who have graced its shores in the last few
decades have called it "lonely" and "creepy." Visitors are allowed on the island if they
can document a family member was buried there.

America as pets but eventually adapted to the climate here and breed in the
wild in New York. They are common visitors to City Island and in nearby
Pelham Bay Park.

While exploring City Island, stop by at **Jack's Bait & Tackle** (551 City
Island Ave.; 718-885-2042; www.jacksbaitandtackle.com) to rent a dingy and
bait for a day of fishing on Manchester Bay. For a bit of history, stop by **The
Nautical Museum** (190 Fordham St.; 718-885-0008; www.cityislandmuseum
.org/) housed inside an old schoolhouse. Exhibits include information on
Thomas Pell, who bought the island in 1654 from the Siwanoy Indians. The
museum is open and free to visitors during weekends from 1 to 5 p.m.

The neighborhood's **Focal Point Gallery** (www.focalpointgallery.com)
showcases photography of local and international artists. Visual workshops
are also available in black and white photography, Photoshop, and amateur
photography. Don't forget to check out what City Island is known for: its
food. For a bite of savory seafood, head to the end of the island to the local
favorite **Johnny's Reef Restaurant** at 2 City Island Ave. (718-885-2086) for
lobster tails, clams, and ice cold beer. Sit outside during warmer months and
watch the island clog with traffic down its lone street leading on and off the
island.

City Island can be tricky to get to for unseasoned tourists. Take the 6
train to Pelham Bay Park and then look for the Bx29 public bus or a New
York taxi. Make sure to check the returning bus schedule posted at the bus
stop when in City Island. The public buses run sporadically to and from the
island.

## Places to Eat in the Bronx

**Ann and Tony's**
2407 Arthur Ave.
(718) 933-1469
www.annandtonysonline
.com

**The Café Sevilla**
1209 White Plains Rd.
(718) 822-9104

**Crab Shanty One**
361 City Island Ave.
City Island
(718) 885-1810
www.originalcrabshanty
.com

**Dominick's Restaurant**
2335 Arthur Ave.
(718) 733-2807

**Frankie And Johnnie's Pine Tavern Restaurant**
1913 Bronxdale Ave.
(718) 792-5956
www.fjpine.com

**Harbor Restaurant**
565 City Island Ave.
(718) 885-1373
www.theharborrestaurant
.com

**Jake's Steakhouse**
6031 Broadway
(718) 581-0182

**Le Refuge Inn**
586 City Island Ave.
(718) 885-2478
www.lerefugeinn.com

**Portofino Restaurant**
555 City Island Ave.
(718) 885-1220
www.portofinocityisland
.com

**Rambling House**
4291 Katonah Ave.
(718) 798-4510

**Riverdale Garden**
4576 Manhattan College
Parkway (242nd Street)
(718) 884-5232
www.riverdalegarden.com

**Roberto's**
603 Crescent Ave.
(718) 733-9503

# BROOKLYN →

Just a few years ago, most tourists wouldn't put Brooklyn on their "to-do-list," but today they arrive by the subway full, spilling into the galleries of Williamsburg, strolling across the Brooklyn Bridge past the iconic brownstones of Brooklyn Heights, lounging by the water in Empire State Park, and hiking the hidden trails in Prospect Park. You could easily devote an entire New York City vacation to Brooklyn and never run out of neighborhoods, parks, restaurants, and art to explore.

Brooklyn was once inhabited by the Lenape Native Americans, meaning "the People" and included the Nayack and Canarsee tribes. Those familiar with the area may recognize Nayack as the art-centered town called Nyack just west of the city on the Hudson River, and the Carnarsee as present-day Canarsie in Brooklyn. Brooklyn was established as the Dutch town of Breuckelen in 1646, as a nod to its namesake in the Netherlands. The new inhabitants founded the villages of Brooklyn, Bushwick, Flatbush, Flatlands, and New Utrecht, followed by Gravesend. The British eventually took over the area in 1674 and it became Kings County. Today, a close observer to the terrain and layout of the borough may notice the streets in Brooklyn do not always line up. In part, this is because each of the towns was independent and created its own street grids.

As food and supplies passed from Long Island through Brooklyn to New York City, horse-powered ferries and rowboats filled the East River. The U.S. Navy opened a shipyard in 1801 and in just five years, Brooklyn's population doubled to nearly 80,000 as an influx of Irish and German immigrants filled the borough. Eventually, Brooklyn was annexed into New York City in 1898. The borough quickly exploded with industry once the railroads, subway lines, trolleys, and bridges were erected to unify the city. Brooklyn soon became a national leader in sugar refining, gas refineries, ironworks, sweatshops, and factories. After the Great Depression, industry began to crumble and neighborhoods fell into disrepair before a revival struck Brooklyn during the 1980s. Today, the borough houses professionals, artists, families, students, and immigrants seeking opportunity and proximity to Manhattan.

## coldwarartifacts

While the world-famous *Brooklyn Bridge* may not be considered an off-beat attraction, some of its hidden history will spark renewed interest. During a routine inspection in 2006, Cold War era ration supplies were found in a forgotten storeroom nestled in the masonry foundation of the bridge. A cache of calorie-packed crackers, blankets, medical supplies, and water drums were marked with the years 1957, the year the Soviet Sputnik satellite was launched, as well as the year 1962, the year of the Cuban missile crisis.

You can get a postcard view of Brooklyn if you hoof it over from lower Manhattan, and walk across the iconic 1883 Brooklyn Bridge, ranking as one of the great suspension bridges in the world. You'll land in Brooklyn Heights, an upscale, beautiful, and expensive 50-block historic district that served as the backdrop in such films as *Moonstruck* and *Prizzi's Honor.* Among the famous people who have lived in the area: Truman Capote, Walt Whitman, Arthur Miller, Gypsy Rose Lee, Heath Ledger, Michelle Williams, Maggie Gyllenhaal, and Peter Sarsgard.

The bridge continues to draw visitors looking for a leisurely stroll from Brooklyn into Manhattan. You can find a pedestrian walkway entrance leading up a staircase from Cadman Plaza East and Prospect Street, with the Manhattan side spilling out at City Hall. Many tourists labor under the delusion that they will be forced to walk next to the bustle of New York traffic. Walkers and bikers enjoy a separate, elevated walkway while cars travel underneath.

Relatively unexplored by tourists, there is a neighborhood situated directly below the Brooklyn and Manhattan Bridges called *DUMBO,* or Down Under Manhattan Bridge Overpass. It was formerly a seedy neighborhood that only artists and drifters ever graced. Today its coveted real estate sells in the millions and draws young families and professionals by the droves. The neighborhood still retains some of its artistic vibe with local galleries Galapagos Art Space, St. Ann's Warehouse, and Umbrage Gallery among dozens of others.

It's easy to see why the neighborhood got its name. Walk along the waterfront or down Front Street and watch as the Manhattan Bridge boldly straddles the neighborhood, planting itself on bits of uneven cobblestone streets. Subway traffic from the bridge can prove deafening at times, but locals don't seem to notice or mind. Tourists may know the area best as the home of *Grimaldi's Pizza* (19 Old Fulton St., Brooklyn; 718-858-4300; www.grimaldis .com), serving up world-famous pizza that locals line up for. Watch for the line stretching halfway down the block and expect to wait at least a half an hour just to sit down.

For a more upscale meal, try the *River Cafe* (718-522-5200; www.river cafe.com) at 1 Water Street, just a half block away from the world-famous pizzeria. This well-trafficked restaurant features some of the best views in Brooklyn. Sit right along the waterfront and watch Manhattan light up across the East River just after sunset. A prix fixe menu features delicious appetizers, an entree, and dessert. Try the standing chocolate Brooklyn Bridge Marquis cake and tell them you're celebrating a special event—they'll add a special flourish.

The River Cafe is adjacent to the *Fulton Ferry Landing,* the oldest ferry landing in the city. Men once worked to row passengers across the river in the 1600s as a means to connect Brooklyn to Manhattan, and George Washington retreated here after losing the Battle of Long Island. The dock is full of locals looking for an ice cream cone at the Brooklyn Ice Cream factory or a place to catch some sun and watch the boats skip across the river. It's also a popular spot for weddings and tourists hopping on and off New York's water taxis. Although you can take the 2 or 3 train to Clark Street or the A or C to High Street, you'll still have to hike it 10 minutes or so down to the pier, as the subways don't run to this area.

At the landing, look for the gently bobbing *Barge Music* (718-624-2083; www.bargemusic.org), New York's floating concert hall. Resting next to the Fulton Ferry Landing, the barge aims to enhance the cultural life of New York through chamber music. A handful of free concerts are available throughout the year. The barge gently sways as guests soak in the music and views in a cozy setting with hardwood floors and beamed ceilings.

A few blocks north from the Fulton Ferry Landing lies one of my favorite spots in all of Brooklyn, the *Empire-Fulton State Park* and expanding *Brooklyn Bridge Park* (www.brooklynbridgepark.org). A rocky waterfront is framed between the exposed legs of the Manhattan Bridge and entices children to skip rocks and chase pigeons along the shore line. Adults lounge on the large, concrete steps leading to the waterfront, or sprawl on picnic blankets on the nearby lawn. Summer evenings bring free, outdoor movies with a backdrop against a gently lit Brooklyn Bridge.

At Empire-Fulton State Park, look for a small nature trail leading down to the water directly underneath the Manhattan Bridge where dogs can be found chasing after loose balls and taking a dip in the water. From this vantage point, you might notice the old Waring Envelope Factory with its painted name fading against the red brick wall. This particular building boasts unbeatable views of Manhattan and large, sprawling lofts for private residents.

For a bite to eat in DUMBO, *Bubby's* at 1 Main St. (718-222-0666; www.bubbys.com) is ideal for a cold beer or slice of heavenly pie. Try the Chocolate Peanut Butter with an icy Brooklyn Lager. The views of Manhattan are also stunning from a window seat on the ground floor. If pie doesn't sound appetizing, the *Jacques Torres Chocolate Factory* at 66 Water St. (718-875-9772; www.mrchocolate.com) will also satisfy your sweet tooth. Sip on hot chocolate while fresh sweets are made right before your eyes (behind a pane of glass) in the on-site factory. Further into the heart of DUMBO, the *General Store* (111 Front St.; 718-855-5288) serves up snacks, sandwiches, coffee, and beer; and *Superfine* at 126 Front St. (718-243-9005) features a funky urban vibe with daily specials, local art, a sunken bar, and pool tables. Superfine is also an award winner for Best Brunch by Best of New York Awards. Try the stack of pancakes, challah bread French toast, or delectable banana blueberry bread.

For kids and history buffs, stop by to see *Jane's Carousel* at 56 Water St. between Main and Dock Streets (www.janescarousel.com). DUMBO real estate developer David Walentas' wife, Jane, made it a labor of love to meticulously restore the carousel after finding it at an auction in Youngstown, Ohio. Currently on display on Water Street, it will move to its permanent home at the Brooklyn Bridge Park and open to the public for rides in 2010.

DUMBO also hosts a popular *Art Under the Bridge Festival* (www.dumboartfestival.org) each year during the fall. Artists of every medium open their galleries and street-side stands to showcase and sell their work. In the past, quirky parades featuring green-painted performers dancing with sawhorses graced the streets. A pile of bananas, shaped like a pyramid, was also on site near the water's edge. Artists, spoken word performers, and musicians crowd the streets for a chance to perform. The festival seems to get a little tamer each year, but still retains its independent spirit and uniquely DUMBO appeal. Show up to find anything from paintings to handmade jewelry to video multimedia installations. Grab a pamphlet from one of the many galleries or coffee shops and browse through the yearly list of free, open galleries.

## Brooklyn Navy Yard–Admiral's Row

Farther off the beaten path, the *Brooklyn Navy Yard* (www.brooklynnavyyard.org) in Vinegar Hill was founded in 1801 as a shipbuilding center and built its first ship, *The Ohio,* in 1820. Located off of Navy Street, Flushing, and Kent Avenues, the historic neighborhood was dismantled and sold to the city during the 1960s. Stroll through the southeast corner of the yard to see Admiral's Row, once a strip of impressive homes and urban mansions. Over the years they have fallen into disrepair and most are slated to be torn down by the city to make room for development.

Head over to the *Promenade* in Brooklyn Heights off of Remsen Street and Henry for a spectacular view of Manhattan. It's a local favorite, and, speaking as a Brooklyn resident, is home to the very best views of Manhattan. Bring a picnic or book and take a break at one of the many benches, or take a stroll and admire the impressive brownstones and carriage houses lining the walkway.

While you're deciding if the Promenade does in fact offer the best views of Manhattan, look over along the water at the expansion of the Brooklyn Bridge Park (www.brooklynbridgepark.org) just beyond the Brooklyn Queens Expressway. The completed park will stretch along the East River for 1.3 miles from around the Manhattan Bridge to Atlantic Avenue. If you're visiting the city during the summer, look for the floating swimming pool at Pier 5, housed on a barge right in the East River. The pool fills up quickly, waits are common, and wall-to-wall swimmers politely skirt past each other. But city views from the deck are truly spectacular.

Just a few blocks from the Promenade, *Clark's Diner* at 80 Clark St. and Henry (718-855-5484) is undeniably one of the best spots for a quick, delicious, and cost-effective breakfast featuring crisp waffles with strawberries, omelets, freshly squeezed orange juice, stacks of mouth-watering pancakes, and hearty sausages. You can also stop in for lunch for sandwiches, soup, and salads. This family-owned restaurant fondly knows their regulars by name, remembers their patron's favorite orders, and is frequented by an occasional Brooklyn celebrity. Stop in and ask for Mark.

Stroll down Henry Street from Clark's down to Montague Street to explore rows of brownstones, architectural gems, churches, and the 19th-century European charm of Brooklyn Heights. The neighborhood is often referred to as "America's first suburb" and was the first neighborhood protected by the city's 1965 Landmark Preservation Law. To see a prime piece of the neighborhood's historic prowess, stop at the corner of Montague and Clinton Street to step inside the majestic building home to Chase Bank. The Italian High Renaissance style building once served as the Brooklyn Trust Company. Once inside, look up at the ornately designed ceiling. Don't worry about looking foolish, the bank tellers are accustomed to it. The Trader Joe's on Atlantic and Court Street rests in another landmark building and former bank.

Also off Montague and Clinton, *St. Ann Holy Trinity Church* at 157 Montague St. (718-975-6960) boasts a Gothic revival style with some of the country's oldest stained glass windows. The church's *St. Ann Center for Restoration and the Arts* was founded in 1988. Its aim is to restore the glass William J. Bolton created for the church between 1844 and 1848 and train new artisans and apprentices with a focus on conservation.

Montague Street is also lined with a handful of chain stores, book shops, family-owned restaurants, pubs, coffee shops, and boutiques. Walk from Court Street down to the Promenade to window shop or find a brunch spot on a Sunday afternoon. For a cold drink off the beaten path, try *Montero's Bar and Grill* (718-624-9799; monterosbar.com) at 73 Atlantic Ave. off of Henry Street in Brooklyn Heights. Their slogan, "We're all here because we're not all there," invites customers into a dive dating back to 1947. Once inside the family–owned bar, check out the collection of nautical-themed décor including life preservers, model ships, and sailor memorabilia.

Tourists can't say they truly know New York without some understanding of its intricate, and seemingly overcomplicated, subway system. Get to know the underground with a visit to the *New York Transit Museum* at Boerum Place and Schermerhorn Street, featuring over 150 years of rapid transit in the city. Photos, maps, documents, subway cars, and subway art fill the museum. An entire section is devoted to abandoned stations that are no longer in operation or accessible to the public. Most locals have never even seen inside the Brooklyn Bridge Local and Express Platforms, the South Ferry Inner Loop, or the 42nd Street Lower Level stops.

The museum (212-878-0106; www.nycsubway.org) is open from Tuesday through Friday 10 a.m. to 4 p.m., and weekends from noon to 5 p.m.; it is closed on Monday and major holidays. Admission runs $5 for adults and $3 for students, children ages 3 to 17, and senior citizens 62 years and older. Seniors also visit free on Wednesday. To get to the museum, take the 2, 3, 4, or 5 trains to Borough Hall, the M, R to Court Street, the A, C, G to Hoyt-Schermerhorn Street, or the A, C, F to Jay Street-Borough Hall.

It is possible to see one of the city's forgotten subway lines in person. Take an underground tunnel tour on Atlantic Avenue and Court Street. The Atlantic Avenue Tunnel was built in 1844 and is officially the world's oldest subway tunnel. The tunnel was thought to be a thing of legends, with stories of

pirates hiding bounty, German saboteurs plotting their revenge, and bootleggers distilling from the underground persisting over the years. But local Bob
Diamond rediscovered the lost tunnel in 1980 after the city continued to claim
it did not exist.

Now the president of the Brooklyn Historic Rail Association, Diamond
leads a tour through the forgotten tunnel. Not for the claustrophobic, the tour
winds through the depths of the half-mile long tunnel. Be aware that the tour
descends directly down a manhole on Atlantic Avenue in Brooklyn Heights
to access the tunnel. I always know the hidden tour is in full force by the
orange safety cones neatly placed around the manhole on a heavily trafficked
Atlantic Avenue. Make sure to wear comfortable shoes and sneakers and call
ahead to (718) 941-3160 for reservations, or visit www.brooklynrail.net for
more information.

Past the area of Brooklyn Heights lie the blurred boundaries of the neighborhoods of Cobble Hill and Carroll Gardens. The quaint, family-oriented
neighborhoods blend children's boutiques with restaurants, bars, coffee shops,
a movie theater, and chain stores. If you're walking down Clinton Street away
from Brooklyn Heights, stop at Verandah Place, resting next to a small urban
park. Make your way down Verandah Place in either direction. While you
won't see any verandahs on Verandah Place, you will see charming carriage
houses lining the street, a lasting remnant to the culture of the 1800s. The carriage houses were usually situated on the same lot as the brownstones behind
them or next door, and operated as livery stables and servant quarters. Over
the years, the brownstones and carriage houses were sold off separately and
eventually restored.

Thomas Wolfe rented an apartment at 40 Verandah Place around the
period he wrote *A Portrait of Bascom Hawke*. Some of my favorite carriage

## Exploring Red Hook

Over in Red Hook, visitors explore galleries, boutiques, and restaurants leading down
to the water's edge. An IKEA opened in 2008 and offers free shuttle service to the
subways, and a water taxi ride to Manhattan for $5, free for kids under 12 and for
those who spend $10 or more at IKEA. At the nearby Pathmark, make your way to
the very back to the deli area and order a sandwich and coffee. Exit to the patio and
sit at a picnic table for views of the Statue of Liberty. Other stops in Red Hook: Eric
Basin for jewelry and furniture at 388 Van Buren St., the funky wireworks and jewelry
shop at Metal and Thread at 398 Van Buren St., and Flickinger Glassworks housing
enameled glass art and tableware.

houses in Brooklyn face each other on Pacific Street between Court and Clinton. The house situated on the eastern side boasts green ivy winding up a white facade and trimmed windows.

***The Gowanus Canal*** (www.gowanus.org) is still gaining a foothold as a local contender to the now mainstream-hip Williamsburg. But, for now, the canal's current real estate prices make it more affordable than living in the neighboring pockets of Carroll Gardens or Park Slope. Although the Gowanus Bay splinters throughout other neighborhoods including Red Hook and Sunset Park, the canal's unique, sideways sliding drawbridge is situated on Carroll Street between Nevins and 3rd Avenue near Carroll Gardens. Locals wait as the drawbridge swings aside for sailboats passing by, one of only four in the country that operates as a retractile bridge.

The canal was once integral to Brooklyn's industry and transported supplies for coal manufacturing, machine shops, chemical plants, sulfur makers, and more. After the construction of the Brooklyn-Queens Expressway (or BQE for locals), the canal's usefulness declined. In the 1960s, a pump broke that served to flush water through the canal. The city ignored the problem for nearly forty years and the canal became a haven for pollution and waste. Bacteria, gonorrhea, typhoid, cholera, and a pungent odor plagued the canal for years before the pump was finally fixed. Today, wildlife has returned to the area including geese, swans, ducks, and crabs. While the water now flows, it's not unusual to see dead jellyfish floating by, or a whiff of pollution wafting past on a hot day.

While developers look to bring condos to the area and turn the Gowanus into a mini Venice Canal, there is still a long way to go before it becomes an upscale waterside oasis. For now, visitors can explore the canal with a canoe with the ***Gowanus Dredgers*** (www.gowanuscanal.org). The group will also assist if you want to launch your own kayak or boat.

Just beyond the drawbridge on Carroll Street lies a squat, urban lighthouse on the shores of the canal. The grounds are dubbed "The Yard" (off of the Gowanus Drawbridge on Carroll Street between Bond Street and Nevins Street; www.bklynyard.com) and feature music and events during the summer months. Frugal visitors can sit along the drawbridge with a slice from a nearby pizzeria or play Frisbee in the street while enjoying music for free.

Year-round, head to the nearby ***Bell House*** at 149 7th St., Brooklyn (718-643-6510; www.thebellhouseny.com) for live music and drinks. The venue was converted from a 1920s factory and features 25-foot wooden arched ceilings and a 450-square-foot stage. Past events included the Cheese Experiment, The Comedians of Law and Order, and The Love Hangover. To reach the Gowanus Canal area, take the F or G trains to Carroll Street, the R or M to Union Street, or the F and G trains to Smith and 9th Streets.

Over in Fort Green, *The Brooklyn Tabernacle* is a full-functioning, active church that began with a handful of members and has now grown into 10,000. Lead by Pastor Cymbala, his wife, Carroll, directs the Grammy-winning Brooklyn Tabernacle Choir. She's also the daughter of the church founder, the late Rev. Clair Hutchins, and started her choir with nine people. Carroll cannot read or write music, but says the Holy Spirit allows her to direct and create music.

Nearly 300 church members sing in the choir, almost all of whom are vocally untrained. The church boasts that their choir members are lawyers, nurses, street people, ex-addicts, and all-around everyday people. The eclectic Brooklyn Tabernacle Choir recently released an album entitled "I'll Say 'Yes'" and has performed at Carnegie Hall, Radio City Music Hall, the Paramount Theater, and a sold-out performance at the Madison Square Garden Theater.

Because of the size of the choir and difficulty in being mobile for ministry, a core group of vocalists called The Brooklyn Tabernacle Singers travels frequently and visits Korea, Japan, and dozens of domestic cities each year. Check the Web site for ongoing services and concerts. Find the Brooklyn Tabernacle at 17 Smith St. Call (718) 290-2000 or visit www.brooklyntabernacle.org.

Brooklyn's neighborhood of Fort Greene has its own glassblowing center, *Urban Glass.* Students learn how to blow glass, make glass beads, and refine their craft. Intensive weekend workshops are also available for locals and visitors stopping through the area. I took a glass bead making class a few years ago and learned to patiently melt down glass spindles without letting it get too hot to pop off or burn. (I spent a lot of time dodging hot, popping, glass.) The softened glass was then carefully woven around steel spindles and gently crafted into beads.

Urban Glass is located at 647 Fulton St., Brooklyn (718-625-3685; www .urbanglass.org). While the facility has various galleries open from 10 a.m. to 5 p.m. from Tuesday through Friday, check the Web site for ongoing open houses, exhibitions, and classes. To get to Urban Glass, take the B, M, Q, or R to DeKalb Avenue, the C to Layfayette Avenue, or the 2, 3, 4, or 5 trains to the Nevins Street Station.

Over in *Fort Greene Park* (fortgreenepark.org), look for a fifteen-story granite column with a metal urn resting at its top. This is the nearly forgotten site of the Fort Greene Park's Prison Ship Martyrs Memorial dating back to the Revolutionary War era. During the war, the British arrested and imprisoned anyone who would not swear allegiance to the Crown of England. They quickly ran out of room in their prison and began housing their American POWs in prison ships floating on the East River. It's estimated that nearly 11,000 people died on the ships from rampant disease and deplorable conditions.

As bones and remains washed up on shore over the years, traumatized Brooklynites carefully collected them to honor their memory and lay their lost soldiers to rest. The remains were put into a hilltop crypt in the present day Fort Green Park. Eventually, a staircase and eternal flame surrounded the pole, immortalizing the forgotten prisoners during the early 1900s.

The history of the pole was mostly forgotten through the generations, the United States started liking the British again, and the staircase was closed. In 2008, the Prison Ship Martyrs Memorial was finally restored after many false starts and two other preservation efforts. Rumor has it that some of the bodies remaining in the crypt were actually identified and only people who can document their blood relation can visit.

Today, the park also hosts greenmarkets, artisan markets, a Tree Trail, playground, tennis court, basketball court, and recreation. To get to the park, take the C to Lafayette, G to Fulton Street; R, Q, B to Dekalb Avenue; or the 2, 3, 4, 5, D, or N trains to Atlantic Avenue.

The popular **Brooklyn Academy of Music** (www.bam.org) features the work of local and international artists and features cinema, fine arts, festivals, dance, literature, lectures, and more. BAM Rose Cinemas features independent films. If you're already familiar with BAM as a well-worn favorite and want to catch a movie and then a bite, try some of the best barbeque around at **The Smoke Joint** (87 South Elliot Place; 718-707-1011; www.thesmokejoint.com) in Fort Greene. Order the mac & cheese the moment you sit down, they often run out as the night wears on. Try the pulled pork sandwiches, crispy catfish, Brooklyn wings, spicy french fries, and spare ribs and then promptly slather on the BBQ and dipping sauces. **The Pig Bar,** adjacent to The Smoke Joint, features tasty micro-brews and artisan whiskeys, bourbon, rye, and wheat. To get to BAM and The Smoke Joint, take the 2, 3, 4, 5, B, or Q to Atlantic

## A Brooklyn Bargain

There is so much going on in Brooklyn that the cultural partnership known as the Heart of Brooklyn finally issued the **Brooklyn Pass,** a two-day passport to the borough's most popular attractions. Priced at $25 ($15 for children), the pass provides admission to the Brooklyn Museum, Brooklyn Botanic Garden, Brooklyn Children's Museum, Prospect Park (Carousel and Independence Electric Boat), Prospect Park Zoo, New York Aquarium, New York Transit Museum, Weeksville Historic Hunterfly Road Houses, and the Jewish Children's Museum. Also included: discounts on food and retail outlets. The pass can be purchased at the South Street Seaport, the Brooklyn Bridge Marriott, and the Brooklyn Tourism and Visitors Center at Brooklyn Borough Hall (209 Joralemon St.) or online at www.brooklynpass.com.

Avenue, the C to Lafayette Avenue, the G to Fulton Street, or the N, R, D, or M to Pacific Street.

For New York–savvy tourists who are well versed with the lush landscape of the gardens, visit the Botanic Garden for a local-favorite event, the annual Sakura Matsuri Cherry Blossom Festival. Held each year over a weekend during spring, the festival offers Seasonal Highlights Tours, over fifty performances, demonstrations, exhibits, and food and drink vendors. It's a beautiful way to spend a Saturday afternoon and take in some of the city's softer side.

After a $3 million restoration, the country's first public Japanese garden provides an exotic refuge in the middle of Brooklyn. Designed in 1915 by Takeo Shiota, the Japanese Hill-and-Pond Garden at the Brooklyn Botanic Garden is an urban retreat like no other in the metropolitan area. Visitors enter through an orange-red Torii gate into a magical world of azaleas, pines, and weeping cherry trees, where dwarf bamboo and irises edge a pond inhabited by bronze cranes and waterfalls cascade gently from recessed grottoes.

*The Brooklyn Botanic Garden,* 1000 Washington Ave., Brooklyn (718-623-7200; www.bbg.org), is open in spring and summer, Tuesday through Friday 8 a.m. to 6 p.m.; weekends and holidays 10 a.m. to 6 p.m. Fall and winter hours are Tuesday through Friday 8 a.m. to 4:30 p.m.; weekends and holidays 10 a.m. to 4:30 p.m. Closed Monday, except on holiday Mondays, and closed major holidays. Admission is $8 for adults, $4 for seniors and students, and free for children 12 and under. Admission is also free each Tuesday, on Saturday from 10 a.m. to noon, on weekdays from mid-November through February, and senior citizens are also admitted free on Friday.

At the *Brooklyn Museum,* 200 Eastern Parkway, Brooklyn (718-638-5000; www.brooklynmuseum.org), which has one of the finest Egyptian collections in the world, there's an outdoor sculpture garden devoted to artwork and architectural details removed from vanished New York City buildings. Here you'll find Adolph Weinman's *Night,* an allegorical female figure carved from pink granite. Along with a companion named *Day,* she once drowsed against a massive clock at one of the entrances to McKim, Mead, and White's magnificent Pennsylvania Station, built in 1910 and lost to developers in 1963.

Look for the 30-foot replica of the Statue of Liberty commissioned in 1900 by Russian auctioneer William H. Flattau. He placed it on top of his eight-story Liberty Warehouse at 43 West 64th Street on the Upper West Side. The replica was restored and given to the Brooklyn Museum, now on display in its outdoor sculpture garden. Museum hours are Wednesday through Friday from 10 a.m. to 5 p.m., and Saturday and Sunday from 11 a.m. to 6 p.m. The first Saturday of each month is open from 11 a.m. to 11 p.m. Suggested contribution is $10 for adults; seniors and students, $6. Take the 2 or 3 trains to Eastern Parkway-Brooklyn Museum stop.

The Brooklyn Museum and Brooklyn Botanic Garden also teamed up to offer a special discount to patrons hitting both attractions. The Brooklyn Art and Garden ticket runs $16 for an adult combo ticket and $9 for seniors and students.

Explore an offbeat kind of green space in Sunset Park's **Green-Wood Cemetery** at 500 25th St. (718-728-7300; www.green-wood.com). The cemetery was founded in 1838 as one of the first rural cemeteries in the country. It's one of the world's most beautiful cemeteries and a National Historic Landmark with a harbor view and 478 acres rich with flowering shrubs, trees, and lakes. Among the some 600,000 people buried here (nearly double the population of Pittsburgh) are Leonard Bernstein, Samuel Morse, Louis Comfort Tiffany, F. A. O. Schwarz, "Boss" Tweed, and mob boss Joey Gallo. Guided tours are offered during the Halloween season and at other times during the year; call to check schedule. To get to the historic cemetery, take the R train to 25th Street.

## trashbecomes treasure

The Brooklyn Botanic Garden was founded in 1910 on the site of an ash dump. It now features 12,000 plant species from throughout the world.

After a few hours exploring Brooklyn, head to Atlantic Avenue for some of the best Middle Eastern food in the city. Get the fresh-baked pita bread and baklava from the **Damascus Bakery** at 195 Atlantic Ave. (718-625-7070), and olives and sumac and all sorts of prepared delicacies from **Sahadi's,** 187 Atlantic Ave. (718-624-4550; www.sahadis .com). Then it's lunch or dinner at the **Tripoli Restaurant** at 156 Atlantic Ave. (718-596-5800; www.tripolirestaurant.com), where authentic Lebanese dishes are modestly priced; entrees start at under $10 and the traditional *mazza,* consisting of twenty mouth-watering dishes, is $41.95.

Atlantic Avenue also features rows of antique shops, galleries, jewelry stores, and boutiques. Among my favorite spot is **Sterling Place** (718-797-5667; www.sterlingplace.com) at 363 Atlantic Ave. between Hoyt and Bond Streets. The shop teems with antique and vintage-style furniture, clocks, handcrafted items, unique gifts, and housewares. Husband and wife team Robert Wilson and Elizabeth Crowell have an eye for tasteful, functional, and often quirky items for display. Stepping inside their shop feels like you've happened upon a curator's exhibit full of handmade rosewood bookcases from India, antique sled repurposed as a coffee table, red leather jewelry boxes delicately finished in beeswax, English armoires, custom made oak dining tables, and one of a kind items you will seldom find anywhere else. Elizabeth and Robert can also give you tips on taking care of your antiques, help find gift items, and give insight to aspiring collectors. In addition to being generous and friendly with their customers, they offer prices fit for any shopper, ranging from a few dollars to the thousands. There's also a second Sterling Place location in Park Slope at 352 7th Avenue and 10th Street.

**The Grand Prospect Hall** is a building with a history. When it was built in 1892, it was the tallest building in Brooklyn, and its French birdcage elevator was Brooklyn's first passenger elevator. William Jennings Bryan also appeared on stage when he was stumping for the presidency, and famous performers that have performed there include Enrico Caruso, Mae West, Lena Horne, and Fred Astaire.

The French Empire–style Victorian confection features a breathtaking lobby, marble grand staircase, rococo-style gold-leafed opera theater, a domed ceiling, and a grand ballroom that can accommodate up to 2,000 people.

Throughout the years, the hall has served as a music hall, a German opera house, a vaudeville theater, a dance hall, a boxing arena, and a professional basketball court. Today it is used as a convention center as well as a venue for weddings, meetings, and bar mitzvahs. The Grand Prospect Hall is located at 263 Prospect Ave., Brooklyn (718-788-0777; www.grandprospect.com). By subway, take the R train to Prospect Avenue.

If you've already explored Central Park and want a comparable and unique alternative, try the 585-acre urban oasis of **Prospect Park** (718-965-8951; www.prospectpark.org) in Brooklyn. Situated near Park Slope, the park houses the only forest in Brooklyn. It's also home to a zoo, lake, old-fashioned carousel, picnic house, playgrounds, tennis, ice skating rink, band shell, baseball fields, horseback riding, and more.

Nature lovers will appreciate the intricate trails leading past waterfalls and wetland, as well as woodland, habitats. Locals come to escape the city and surround themselves in the thick forest canopy. You can easily pass through miles of park without seeing the surrounding buildings and shops, making it a favorite haunt for picnics and romantic getaways. During your nature hike, stop off at the largest rustic shelter in the park, the Arbor. Visitors can follow along with the interpretive trail signs or pick up audio and print materials at the Boat House for a self-guided tour.

Over by the carousel, Prospect Park Zoo, and "Children's Corner," lies the **Lefferts Historic House.** The home was built by a Dutch family in the 18th century in what was once the farming village of Flatbush. The house reflects Brooklyn's pre-Colonial period and features a working garden, documents, period rooms, historic toys, and exhibits. Ongoing programs including candle making, sewing, and butter churning are popular with families.

My favorite spot in Prospect Park is the nation's first urban Audubon Center. *The Prospect Park Audubon Center* is located inside a 1905 Beaux Arts structure and New York City landmark. Arches, tiles, and a balcony were inspired by the architecture of a 16th-century Venetian library. The house also serves as the park's information center and headquarters for electric boat tours along the Lullwater. The center offers interactive exhibits and nature education, and holds special events year-round.

During the summer months, *Celebrate Brooklyn* (www.bricartsmedia .org) offers free films, performances, and concerts drawing jazz, pop, and mainstream musicians from around the world. Past performances included Lincoln Center Jazz Orchestra, David Byrne, and Blonde Redhead. There's a suggested donation at the door, but many locals bring blankets and snacks and sit outside the gate to enjoy the music and lounge away from the intensity of the crowds. The park is closed between 1 and 5 a.m. The F, 2, 3, Q, S, and B all go to the park; check the Prospect Park Web site for more information to specific attractions.

Also near Prospect Park, *The Brooklyn Society for Ethical Culture* at 53 Prospect Park West (718-768-2972; www.bsec.org) offers performances at the Good Coffeehouse Music Parlor, lectures, and fellowship programs. According to their Web site, the center "is a humanistic religious and educational fellowship promoting knowledge, love and practice of ethics-centered living."

The society's headquarters lie in an urban mansion across the street from Prospect Park on an avenue once known as "The Gold Coast" for its impressive buildings and private homes. Architecture buffs take note of the rare neo-Jacobean style and its private garden, the largest of its kind in the city.

The building is rented out for events and weddings year-round and features an impressive Grand Parlor, Garden Room, Billiard Room, and Library. Bluegrass jamborees are common in the garden, and Irish fiddlers or urban

## Christmas in Brooklyn

During the holiday season, *Dyker Heights,* Brooklyn, is renowned for its spectacular light display along a mile stretch of urban homes. Dubbed "the miracle mile," locals and visitors show up by foot and in cars to take in the sights on 84th between 10th and 12th Avenues. Neighbors participate in a friendly competition and erect animated toy soldiers, motorized dolls, miniature villages, and detailed dioramas of the film *Scrooge.* The neighborhood has turned into such a notorious holiday haunt that the NYPD has to help control traffic.

funk jams frequently pop up on the events roster. Tickets to events are reasonable and generally family-friendly.

If you're traveling with children between the ages of 2 and 10, head over to the **Brooklyn Children's Museum.** Founded in 1899, it was the first museum in the world designed expressly for kids. Their philosophy is "touch and learn," so kids can have (relatively) uninhibited fun with a collection of more than 27,000 artifacts and specimens throughout ten galleries. Housed in a unique 35,000-square-foot underground structure, the museum features a turn-of-the-twentieth-century kiosk entrance and a "stream" running the length of the "people tube," a huge drainage pipe that connects four levels of exhibit space. A $39 million expansion doubled the museum's size to 102,000 square feet, and added new galleries and a Kid's Cafe, and became the first "green" museum in the city certified by the Leadership in Energy and Environmental Design (LEED) program.

The Brooklyn Children's Museum is located at 145 Brooklyn Ave., Brooklyn (718-735-4400; www.brooklynkids.org) with varying hours depending on the season; general admission s $7.50 per person and free for children under 1 year. By train, take the 3 to Kingston Avenue, the A to Nostrand Avenue, or the C to Kingston/Throop Avenue. Also for kids, **The Jewish Children's Museum** in Brooklyn is an interactive museum exploring Jewish history and heritage. Learn about holidays, biblical history, Israel, and Jewish culture. An art gallery, mini golf course, and craft workshop are on hand at the 50,000-square-foot multimedia enhanced building. The museum is located at 792 Eastern Parkway; call (718) 468-0600 or visit www.jcmonline.org for more information. Tickets run $10 for adults and children.

Discover a forgotten seven-block society hidden within the depths of the Bedford-Stuyvesant area of Brooklyn. Recently only a footnote in the history books, traces of it still remain. In 1838, just eleven years after New York's abolition of slavery, a free African American named James Weeks bought a plot of land in central Brooklyn. Eventually **Weeksville** grew to some 500 residents complete with churches, a school, newspaper, African–American-owned businesses, an orphanage, and an old-age home. It was the second largest pre-Civil War and self-sufficient African-American community, offering communal support and refuge during the Civil War draft riots. Although Weeksville was thought to exist into the 1930s, it was eventually swallowed up by the sprawling area of present-day Bedford-Stuyvesant, or "BedSty" to locals, and essentially disappeared by the 1950s.

In 1968, historian James Hurley discovered a passage about the village of Weeksville in a book called *Brooklyn's Eastern District*. He recruited the help of local pilot Joseph Haynes in an air search for any remaining evidence of the forgotten village. During the search, they uncovered a quirky lane with four dilapidated wooden houses behind an overgrown yard off of Bergen Street, once referred to as Hunterfly Road of Weeksville. The result? The remains of a historic village were hidden in plain site within the confines of modern buildings and new roads. The discovery was almost too late, as the area was slated for imminent demolition for a new city housing project.

An archaeological dig was quickly organized and conducted by locals, Boy Scouts, school children, and anyone who would lend a hand. Artifacts were uncovered including a tintype photograph of a woman dubbed "The Weeksville Lady," and soon an entire way of life was rediscovered. Through public support, the four Hunterfly Road Houses were declared New York City landmarks in the 1970s and landed on the National Register of Historic Places.

Ongoing public tours unearth how African Americans lived during the 19th and early 20th centuries including a 1930s era kitchen, historical reproductions of decor, and insight into the citizens of Weeksville. Ask your guide about the first African-American woman doctor in New York, Susan Smith-McKinney. The historic Hunterfly Houses are located at present-day 1698 Bergen St. Tours are available Tuesday through Friday at 1 p.m., 2 p.m., and 3 p.m., on Saturday from 11 a.m. to 2 p.m. Admission runs $4 for adults and $1 for students and seniors. Call (718) 756-5250 or visit www.weeksvillesociety .org for more information. Take the subway to A or C to Utica Avenue or the 3, 4 to Crown Height-Utica Avenue.

Williamsburg, historically known as a tight-knit Hasidic neighborhood, has spawned a pocket known for its rapidly growing population of "hipsters" and artists. To peruse the shops, bars, and boutiques that has made Williamsburg a magnet for 20-something-year-old "hipsters," take the L to Metropolitan Avenue from Manhattan and walk down Bedford near 7th Street and get to know the area by foot.

One of the most famous residents of Williamsburg is the local brew, Brooklyn Lager. The line of popular Brooklyn beers made its home at the **Brooklyn Brewery** at 79 North 11th St. (718-486-7422; brooklynbrewery.com) and it all began in 1987 by Steve Hindy, a former Associated Press correspondent, and Tom Pottter, former lending officer at Chemical Bank. Hindy started learning the beer brewing process and the new partners first brewed a test batch, hand-labeled in the basement of their Brooklyn brownstone. They came up with their logo for Brooklyn Beer after hiring graphic designer Milton Glaser, best known as the creator of the logo for the I Love New York campaign. The partners started their own distribution company to transport and market their beers across New York. After years of brewing their brand upstate, they eventually bought a former matzo ball factory in Williamsburg, Brooklyn, and converted it into Brooklyn Brewery.

Visitors can imbibe from the enormous vats of brews like Monster Ale and Brooklyn Brown on Friday night from 6 to 11 p.m., but for hops enthusiasts there are ongoing free hourly tours on weekends between 1 and 4 p.m. Take the L train to Bedford Avenue. If you want to keep imbibing on a budget, head to 600 Metropolitan Ave. to the *Alligator Lounge* (718-599-4440) for a small brick-oven pizza free with every beer you purchase.

*McCarren Park Pool* (www.mccarrenpark.com) opened in 1936 in the middle of the Great Depression during a series of ten pool openings in the city in hopes of generating jobs and offers locals recreational relief. McCarren Park pool cost $1 million and was the size of three Olympic-sized pools for a capacity of 6,800 swimmers, making it one of the largest public pools in the world.

Over the years, the pools fell into disrepair and eventually closed by the 1980s. Despite attempts to fix it up, locals protested over the crime it would draw, and a divisive community erupted. The pool was eventually cleaned up, but not as a swimming hole. Over the years, it was used for concerts and events, giving spectators a unique angle of looking up at the stage with hardly a bad "seat" in the house. Patrons walked around and watched impromptu games of dodge ball and slip-and-slide-style water games break out before heading to neighboring bars like Enid's and Matchless. For more popular concerts, lines around the pool doubled, making it difficult to gain entry. The efforts to raise money were a success, and as of 2010, the pool is slated to be a swimming hole once again. Upcoming summer concerts are moving over to the East River between North Eighth and North Ninth Streets in Williamsburg. To visit the pool, take the L train to Bedford Avenue or Lorimer; or the G to Metropolitan Avenue stop.

After a hot day at the pool, stop by *Pete's Candy Store* at 709 Lorimer St. (718-302-3770; www.petescandystore.com) for a beer, open mic, live entertainment, Pete's Reading Series,—or church. (Church in a bar with brews: the way some Brooklynites think it should be.) Jay Bakker sets up shop on Sunday afternoons for "Revolution Church" directly inside the bar. If the name Bakker sounds familiar, it might be because his parents are Jim and Tammy Faye. After their ex-communication from the church in the late 1980s, Jay spent years battling substance abuse and reevaluating religion. He got his life back together and organized his grassroots efforts at a bar in Atlanta before he and his wife settled in New York City. To get to Pete's take the L train to Bedford Avenue or the G train to Metropolitan.

For a look at local work on the cheap, try *SK Art* at 39 Guernsey St. (stevekeene.com/sksk.html) in Williamsburg. Only open on Sunday from 2 to 6 p.m. or by appointment, SK Art features the work of local artist Steve

Keene. This isn't like any other gallery you've probably ever been in. Walk in to find a haphazard heap of rows of wooden canvases. Keene wanted art to be cheap and accessible and likens the process to a CD: "It's cheap, it's art and it changes your life, but the object has no status. Musicians create something for the moment, something with no boundaries and that kind of expansiveness is what I want to come across in my work," says his Web site. Keene is known for creating one-of-a-kind artwork, but in multiples on wooden canvases and has produced CD covers for the bands Pavement, The Apples in Stereo, Dave Mathews Band, The Victoria Lucas, and Soul Coughing. He also features quirky items including wooden cutouts of painted pretzels, fruits, surfers, and household objects. Take the G train to Nassau Avenue or the L to Bedford.

Although there are plenty of artists living in Williamsburg and the neighborhood teems with independent galleries, there are few large art centers to be found. Try the *Williamsburg Art and Historical Center* at 135 Broadway (718-486-7372; www.wahcenter.net), or WAH. Located in the landmark Kings County Savings Bank, the center was founded in 1996 by artist and philanthropist Yuko Nii. The building itself is a work of art and is renowned for having a spot on the National Register of Historic Places. WAH Center regularly hosts art exhibitions, performances, and cultural events as well as lectures, seminars, and educational programs. The organization takes as much interest in preserving its historical building as it does its art and artifacts on display. The gallery is open on weekends from noon to 6 p.m. or by appointment. Admission varies depending on the event, but ranges from $3 to $10. Take the L train to Bedford, or the J, M, Z to Marcy Avenue.

## harbormuseum

Brooklyn is home to the city's only active military post, U.S. Army Fort Garrison. On site, the *Harbor Museum* showcases United States' army weapons, uniforms, cannons, and historical artifacts. The museum, located at 230 Sheridan Loop in the Fort Hamilton area in Bay Ridge, is open Monday through Friday 10 a.m. to 4 p.m., and Saturday from 10 a.m. to 2 p.m. and offers free admission. Call ahead, advance reservations are required. Take the R train to 95th Street. Call (718) 630-4349 or visit www.harbordefensemuseum .com for more information.

Touching the Atlantic Ocean, Coney Island is home to *The Wildlife Conservation Society's New York Aquarium* (www.nyaquarium.com). It is the oldest continuously operating aquarium in the country and is home to more than 10,000 specimens, including the only California sea otters outside of California, and the only aquarium-born beluga whales to survive past their first birthday.

The aquarium's Sea Cliffs, a 300-foot-long re-creation of the rocky Pacific coast, is now home to walruses; harbor, grey, and fur seals; sea otters; and black-footed penguins. Exhibits in Conservation Hall focus on the society's efforts to protect marine species around the world, replicating habitats in areas such as the Belize Barrier Reef, the Amazon River, the Coral Reef, and Lake Victoria. The Aquatheater features a 200,000-gallon pool where marine mammal demonstrations are held throughout the day.

The New York Aquarium, Surf Avenue and West 8th Street (718-265-FISH), is open daily at 10 a.m.; closing hours vary, from 4:30 p.m. to 7 p.m. Admission runs $13 for adults, $9 for children (ages 3-12), and seniors (age 65+) $10. For frugal travelers, there is a pay-as-you-wish donation on Friday at 3 p.m. Take the F or Q trains to the West 8th Street station in Coney Island or the N or D to Coney Island-Stillwell Avenue Station.

The amusement park that made *Coney Island* famous in the 1920s is long gone. The wooden boardwalk and a handful of rides that remain are dim reminders of its glory days, as are the famous freak shows that once titillated the throngs on a summer's night. Despite its fading foothold in garish circus culture, freak show performances are still common along the boardwalk with performers calling themselves Donny Vomit, Serpentina, and Jackie the Human Tripod.

Still standing in full force is the *Coney Island Museum,* at 208 Surf Ave., a small but unusually engaging collection of Coney Island memorabilia. It's really just a random collection of antiques and photographs about forgotten rides. The museum is small, a work in progress, but it gives visitors a glimpse into the Coney Island of long ago, including Luna Park. The park was open from 1903 to 1946 when it caught on fire and was eventually demolished. The former park was home to Topsy, a domestic and cantankerous circus elephant that killed three men in three years. One of her victims was cruel and stupid enough to feed her a lit cigarette, prompting his demise.

The park decided to publicly hang Topsy for her circus crimes, to which the ASPCA promptly protested. By then the city had abandoned hanging in favor of electrocution, and it was decided the elephant would get "the chair." (Apparently, the ASPCA found this an acceptable and more humane alternative.) The story gets stranger. Thomas Edison, who owned patents relating to his findings with direct currents and electricity, wanted to scorch his competition. George Westinghouse and Nicola Tesla had come out with an alternating current technology and Edison wanted to prove its dangers. To make his point, Edison had notoriously filmed a twisted series of electrocutions with stray dogs and cats before agreeing to electrocute poor Topsy, film it, and show it to the public to prove his competitor wrong.

On that fateful day, Topsy was restrained and fitted with wooden sandals laced with copper electrodes. After the park fed the doomed elephant cyanide-laced carrots to ensure she would really die no matter what, she was electrocuted and killed instantly. On January 5, 1903, Thomas Edison filmed the spectacle in front of nearly 1,500 witnesses and promoted the film the following year with the title, *Electrocuting an Elephant.* Alternating current was publicly panned and Edison won his victory. Put a penny into the museum's antique Mutoscope and watch the images unfold Topsy's tragic tale. It really gives you pause to consider Edison was at the helm.

Admission to the Coney Island Museum is a mere ninety-nine cents, and the museum is open Saturday and Sunday from noon to 5 p.m. (sometimes longer hours during summer). Call (718) 372-5159 or visit www.coneyisland .com/museum for more information.

Most tourists head to Coney Island not for the twisted stories of elephant electrocution, but for one of the world's oldest wooden roller coaster: The Cyclone. Climb aboard and in the brief moment when you reach the top of that first hill, take in the breathtaking sites of the Atlantic Ocean and park just below. It quickly disappears as guests plummet down the first bend. The coaster's steep climbs and delicious descents make up for the short ride along the compact coaster.

But there's more to do in Coney Island than just roller coasters and learning about its fading folklore. When the Dodgers left Brooklyn for Los Angeles in 1957, the borough was left without a baseball team. Some say locals never quite got over it and continue to hold a grudge. In 2001, Mayor Giuliani and an ownership group worked to bring the pastime back to the borough. *The Cyclones* (718-449-8497; www.brooklyncyclones.com) played their first game on June 25, 2001. Keyspan Park is also the home of many concerts and provides both field and bleacher seats. Go for stunning nighttime views of the Cyclone roller coaster, the water, and parts of the city twinkling below. Tickets are also a fraction of the cost of a Mets or Yankees game and beer and hot dogs are also considerably cheaper.

Also worth a stop in Coney Island, *Ruby's Old Tyme Bar,* or just Ruby's, is at 1213 Riegelmann right on the boardwalk. A motley crew of beers and beverages can be purchased and sipped outside on picnic tables while overlooking the Atlantic. Snacks are also never far from reach. Nearby vendors serve fried foods ranging from funnel cakes, chicken fingers, corn dogs, burgers, fries, and oysters. If you're visiting during the July 4th holiday, head to *Nathan's Famous* in Coney Island, home of Nathan's International Hog Dog Eating Contest. The spectacle of dozens of hotdogs vanishing within minutes is enough to make you swear off hotdogs for life. Over on Stillwell Avenue, you can also see the Wall of Fame, honoring the champions since 1984 with the motto: "They Came. They Ate. They Conquered."

# The Canarsie Pier

Most tourists never venture far enough into Brooklyn to enjoy *The Canarsie Pier* (www.nyharborparks.org) along the salt marshes of Jamaica Bay. Once a center for commercial fishing, the area was so popular it once featured a floating bath house and summer bungalows. In the 1920s, the water became so polluted the city shut down fishing operations. Today, the water quality has been restored and a 600-foot pier attracts locals and visitors for fishing, rollerblading, jogging, and picnicking.

Seasonally, Coney Island holds a *Mermaid Parade* (https://www.coney island.com) featuring unusual, if not downright garish, costumes. Participants parade down Surf Avenue in mermaid dress while a celebrity King Neptune and Queen Mermaid rule over their subjects. Locals and celebrities come out to gawk, including Queen Latifah and Moby. After the procession, a Mermaid Parade Ball serves as an official after-party to the parade.

For more information about Brooklyn attractions, tours, discounts, and hotels, visit www.visitbrooklyn.org.

## Places to Eat in Brooklyn

**Acqua Santa**
556 Driggs Ave.
(718) 384-9695
www.acquasanta.com

**Al di Là**
248 Fifth Ave.
(718) 636-8888
www.aldilatrattoria.com

**Alma**
187 Columbia St.
(718) 643-5400
www.almarestaurant.com

**Applewood**
501 11th St.
(718) 788-1810
www.applewoodny.com

**Buttermilk**
577 Fifth Ave.
(718) 788-6297
www.buttermilkchannelnyc
.com

**Chestnut**
271 Smith St.
(718) 243-0049
www.chestnutonsmith.com

**Convivium Osteria**
68 Fifth Ave.
(718) 857-1833
www.convivium-osteria
.com

**Egg**
135 N 5th St.
(718) 302-5151
www.pigandegg.com

**Frankie's 457 Spuntino**
457 Court St.
(718) 403-0033
www.frankies457.com

**Franny's**
295 Flatbush Ave.
(718) 230-0221
www.frannysbrooklyn.com

**The Good Fork**
391 Van Brunt St.
(718) 643-6636
www.goodfork.com

**The Grocery**
288 Smith St.
(718) 596-3335

**Junior's (cheesecake)**
386 Flatbush Ave.
(718) 852-5257

**La Lunetta Restaurant**
116 Smith St.
(718) 488-6269
www.lunetta-ny.com

**Peter Luger Steakhouse**
178 Broadway
(718) 387-7400
www.peterluger.com

# QUEENS

→

Queens may be the most ethnically diverse 115 square miles on earth, with the number seven subway line nicknamed "The International Express" and designated a National Millennium Trail for its representation of the immigrant experience.

Dine on authentic Greek fare in Astoria or Peruvian grilled chicken in Jackson Heights. Asian restaurants reflect the large Chinese and Korean population, while Sunnyside offers visitors nightlife at a Spanish theater or a Romanian nightclub. In Woodside, you can rent a Thai video or hear traditional music at an Irish pub. Queens is never short on culture, good food, and art.

The borough has secured a reputation as an important cultural destination. Some of the metropolitan area's most esteemed international art exhibits are hosted at the ***P.S.1 Contemporary Art Center*** in Long Island City (where many of the borough's cultural attractions are located). Housed in a former elementary school, the center is affiliated with Manhattan's Museum of Modern Art (MOMA), but has a much edgier atmosphere. Known for avant-garde exhibits, the recently remodeled facility includes sculpture, a theater, and many modern installations. During exhibition openings, artists who are receiving free workspace in the buildings open their studios to the public, and in summer, DJs spin on the roof. The P.S.1 Contemporary Art Center (718-784-2084; ps1.org) is located at 22–25 Jackson Ave. and is open Monday through Thursday noon to 6 p.m. The museum is closed Tuesday, Wednesday, Thanksgiving, Christmas, and New Year's Day. Suggested donation is $5; $2 for seniors and students. To reach P.S.1, take the E or V trains to the 23rd/Ely Avenue stop, the 7 train to 45th Road and Courthouse Square, or the G train to the 21st Street and Van Alst stop.

"It is said that stone is the affection of old men," said American-Japanese sculptor Isamu Noguchi, explaining his obsession with the medium. Caress the smooth, cold stone of his pieces at the *Isamu Noguchi Garden Museum* (9–01 33rd Rd. at Vernon Boulevard, Long Island City; 718-204-7088; www.noguchi.org), a brick factory building the artist converted for use as a warehouse in the 1970s. Prior to the museum's opening, he added a dramatic open-air addition and an outdoor sculpture garden. Today more than 250 of his works are exhibited in twelve galleries in the building. They include stone, bronze, and wood sculptures; models for public projects and gardens; elements of dance sets designed for choreographer Martha Graham; and Noguchi's Akari lanterns.

Noguchi's major granite and basalt sculptures are displayed in the garden, as is his tombstone, under which half of his ashes are interred. The other half are buried in his garden studio in Japan.

The Isamu Noguchi Garden Museum is open Wednesday through Friday 10 a.m. to 5 p.m., Saturday and Sunday from 11 a.m. to 6 p.m. Admission is $10 for adults and $5 for seniors and students. On the first Friday of every month, you may pay what you wish.

Since the 1920s, hundreds of jazz musicians, including such icons as Dizzy Gillespie, Fats Waller, Billie Holiday, Ella Fitzgerald, and the late, great Louis Armstrong have called Queens home. Armstrong trumpeted his way out of New Orleans as a young man, traveling the world and performing before settling in New York. For nearly thirty years, "Satchmo" looked to Queens as a quiet place where he rested, rehearsed, and spent time with friends and family between recording sessions, club gigs, and concert tours.

Music aficionados head to *Steinway & Sons Piano Factory Tour* in Astoria for an in-depth tour on how pianos were invented in 1711 as a

## weepingbeech park

The first tree to be designated an official landmark by the New York City Landmarks Preservation Commission was the weeping beech tree now in *Weeping Beech Park,* Thirty-seventh Avenue between Parson Boulevard and Bowne Street. It was grown from a cutting taken from a tree at an estate at Beersal, Belgium.

simultaneous percussion and stringed instrument. Travel through the factory to discover how Heinrich Steinway learned furniture making in Germany and eventually applied his meticulous skills to building pianos. His family eventually moved to New York in the mid 1800s and the Steinway factory was born.

Today, thousands of pianos are meticulously crafted in the Queens factory. The workers tell tales of the piano "getting its soul" during the manufacturing process and its resulting music a collaboration between piano player and workers in the shop. One piano might take a year to construct by no fewer than 450 skilled, artisan workers. The documentary *Note by Note* (www.note bynotethemovie.com) follows a Steinway from the forest floor to concert hall.

The Steinway Factory (718-721-2600; www.steinway.com), located at 1 Steinway Place, is open for tours on Monday and Tuesday by appointment. Call in advance for an updated list of upcoming tours and times. By subway, take the N or R to Ditmars Avenue.

For a drink with history, the **Bohemian Hall and Beer Garden** in Astoria, Queens, is the last original remaining beer garden in the city. At one point there was around 800 different beer gardens scattered throughout the boroughs, all of which slowly closed and were sold off.

The remaining Astoria beer garden was built in 1910 and is run by the Bohemian Citizens Benevolent Society in an effort to preserve its history. The bar takes its beer culture seriously and features a selection of Krusovice, Brouczech Staropramen, Czechvar, Erdinger, a variation of American beers, and a full line of wine. The outdoor garden swells with thirsty locals and tourists during summer months, and a line can be found down the block just to get in. Once inside, large picnic tables, live entertainment, and Czech food are on hand for hungry patrons.

Unlike any beer garden I've heard of, the Bohemian Hall also offers a Czech school to children who want to learn the language and culture. The free education features reading, writing, singing, dancing, painting, and drama that reflects the Bohemian culture and lifestyle. Classes take place on Friday from 5 to 7 p.m. for kids ages 6 to 13.

The Bohemian Hall and Beer Garden (718-274-4925; www.bohemianhall .com) is located at 29-19 24th Ave. in Astoria, Queens. The restaurant is open Monday through Wednesday from 5 to 10 p.m., Thursday and Friday from 5 to 11 p.m., and weekends from noon to 11 p.m. Have a drink at the Beer Garden on Monday through Wednesday from noon to 2 a.m., Thursday through Saturday from noon to 3 a.m., and Sunday noon to 2 a.m. Between Memorial Day and Labor Day, the restaurant is open for lunch. By subway, take the N train to Astoria Boulevard.

For low-key casual dining on hotdogs, hamburgers, and standard beers after a day of art in Long Island City, try the **Water Taxi Beach Bar.** Tables sit in 44,000 square feet of sand and locals watch as the sun skirts below the Manhattan skyline. A spontaneous dance party, volleyball match, and games often break out over live entertainment or music blasting from one of the speakers. Kids frequent the bar with their parents and have room to run around. The major downside is the bar is a hike from the subway and the only bathrooms are port-a-potties. Fortunately, the bathrooms are surprisingly clean, and after a few beers, you will hardly care.

The Water Taxi Beach Bar (877-974-6998; www.watertaxibeach.com) opens seasonally around Memorial Day and is closed Monday through Wednesday, open Thursday from 4 to 11 p.m.; Friday 4 p.m. to 2 a.m.; Saturday from noon to 3 a.m.; and Sunday 1 to 10 p.m. Note that the beach turns into a 21 and older spot after 8 p.m. on Friday and Saturday nights and closes for the season in early October. Check the Web site for an updated calendar. Get there by taking the 7 train to Vernon Boulevard/Jackson Avenue or the E train to 23rd Street/Ely Avenue. You can also take a four-minute water taxi directly from midtown Manhattan, which is my preferred method of Beach Bar travel.

## Off to the Races

After the Civil War, the city began building race tracks across the boroughs and brought the elite to neighborhoods like Brighton Beach, Sheepshead Bay, and Coney Island. Many of the city's tracks have since closed, with the exception of a handful tucked into corners tourists rarely frequent.

In Ozone Park the *Aqueduct Race Track,* or just "the Big A" to locals, originally opened on September 27, 1894, under the vision of esteemed racing entrepreneur Arthur Belmont II. The track eventually reopened in 1959 after being torn down and renovated over the years. Today, nearly 40,000 people fill the Aqueduct to watch horses race along a 1⅛ mile Main Course, 1 mile Inner Dirt Course, and a Turf Course. The facilities are also winterized for year-round racing.

The city (unsuccessfully) looked to close down the track in 2007, but the neighborhood lobbied to keep it up and running. The nearby Belmont Race Track in Elmont was slated to absorb the local race traffic instead. The public won, and two-dollar bets are still common while spectators watch as the horses bolt down the tracks to the sound of cheers and stomping from the grandstand. The Backyard also hosts outdoor concerts and family-friendly events throughout the year.

The Aqueduct Race Track (718-641-4700; www.nyra.com) is located at 110-00 Rockaway Blvd.; check the Web site for updated race times and additional information. To catch a race, take the F train to 169th Street or 170th Street and transfer to the N6 or Q2 bus to Belmont, or take the E train to Jamaica Center-Parsons Boulevard and transfer to the Q11 bus to Belmont.

Despite the city's reputation as a concrete jungle, the borough of Queens is never short on nature-inspired activities. Step back in time and get back to the land at the *Queens Country Farm Museum* in Floral Park, Queens. Dating back to 1697, the 47-acre parcel is the only historical working farm in the city and rests on an undisturbed tract of actual farmland. Guests can peruse the greenhouses, livestock, orchard, fields, and an herb garden. City folks who are tired of shoeing away city pigeons and squirrels purchase animal feed at the gift shop to serve resident sheep and goats. Hayrides, summer camps, night walks, apple festivities, and Native American pow-wows are also available during special events throughout the year. It may be hard to believe a working farm exists in the same city as the Empire State Building, but this city is full of eccentric oddities.

The Queens County Farm Museum (718-347-3276; www.queensfarm.org) is located at 73-50 Little Neck Parkway in Floral Park, Queens, and is open Monday through Friday 10 a.m. to 5 p.m. for outdoor visiting only. On weekends, explore the museum and grounds from 10 a.m. to 5 p.m. Until November 1, the interactive corn maze is open from 11 a.m. to 4:30 p.m. and the pumpkin patch from 11 a.m. to 4 p.m. Admission is free, except during special events; check the Web site for a current list and prices. To get there by public transportation, take the E or F train to Kew Gardens/Union Turnpike Station and transfer to the Q46 Bus eastbound to Little Neck Parkway.

*The Louis Armstrong House* in Corona was the legend's modest, two-story home. He and his wife, Lucille, bought the house in 1943, and he lived there until his death in 1971. (Lucille passed away in 1983.) The home is like Graceland for jazz lovers, though instead of the over-the-top décor and extravagance of Elvis' beloved Jungle Room, the Armstrong home is relatively modest and simple—especially considering the wealth the great musician amassed in his lifetime. Lucille's mother lived in a second-story apartment, while Louis and Lucille stayed in a snug one-bedroom on the first floor. When mother passed on, Lucille renovated the home and furnished it with hand-carved Moroccan shutters, bamboo curtains, and a 12-inch color TV set. And since a man's home is his castle, 24 karat gold fixtures can be found in the Armstrong bathroom. While Lucille focused on redecorating, Louis was more interested in collecting audio recordings. Apparently he had an unusual habit of recording everything that went on in his house, including his parties.

Now completely restored and open to visitors, the 1910 house holds a collection of Armstrong memorabilia, including scrapbooks, photos, and gold-plated trumpets. The home's furnishings remain much as they were during Louis and Lucille's lifetimes. A gift shop on the premises sells Armstrong CDs, books, postcards, T-shirts, red beans and rice, and other items.

## OTHER ATTRACTIONS WORTH SEEING IN NEW YORK CITY

**American Museum of Natural History**
Central Park West at 79th Street
(212) 769-5100
www.amnh.org

**Central Park**
Fifth Avenue at 64th Street
(212) 861-6030
www.centralpark.com

**Ellis Island Immigration Museum**
1 Ellis Island
(212) 363-3200
www.nps.gov

**Empire State Building**
350 Fifth Ave. (34th Street)
(212) 736–3100
www.esbnyc.com

**Frick Collection**
1 E. 70th St.
(212) 288-0700
www.frick.org

**Guggenheim Museum**
1071 Fifth Ave.
(212) 423-3500
www.guggenheim.org

**Hispanic Society of America Museum and Library**
613 West 155th St.
(212) 926-2234
www.hispanicsociety.org

**Metropolitan Museum of Art**
1000 Fifth Ave.
(212) 535-7710
www.metmuseum.org

**Museum of Modern Art**
11 West 53rd St.
(212) 708-9400
www.moma.org

**National Academy Museum and School of Fine Arts**
1083 Fifth Ave. (89th Street)
(212) 369-4880
www.nationalacademy.org

**Neue Gallerie**
1040 Fifth Ave. (86th Street)
(212) 628-6200
www.neuegallerie.org

**New York Botanical Garden**
200th Street and Southern Boulevard
(Kazimiroff Boulevard)
(718) 817-8700
www.nybg.org

**St. Patrick's Cathedral**
Fifth Avenue at 50th Street
(212) 753-2261
www.saintpatrickscathedral.org

**Top of the Rock**
30 Rockefeller Plaza
(212) 698-2000
www.topoftherocknyc.com

**Whitney Museum of American Art**
945 Madison Ave.
(212) 570-3600
www.whitney.org

**Zoo/Wildlife Conservation Park**
River Parkway–Fordham Road
(718) 220-5100
www.zoo.org

The Louis Armstrong House, 34–56 107th Street, Corona (718-478-8274; www.satchmo.net), is open Tuesday through Friday 10 a.m. to 5 p.m., Saturday noon to 5 p.m. (last tour at 4 p.m. each day). Admissions run $8 for adults; $6 seniors 65 years and older, students and children; and children 4 and under are free.

Queens is home of both the New York Mets and the U.S. Open Tennis Championship, not to mention two World's Fairs (1939 and 1964). Queens is now home to hundreds of thousands of immigrants; among the earliest was John Bowne, who built *Bowne House* in 1661. Two years after the Bowne House was built, the town meeting of nearby Jamaica offered a bounty of seven bushels of corn for every wolf shot. But wolves weren't the only threat John Bowne faced. As a devoted Quaker, he openly challenged Governor Peter Stuyvesant's edict banning of his religion and began holding meetings of the Society of Friends in his own kitchen. Bowne was arrested and sent back to Europe in 1662 but returned to New York two years later, after being exonerated by the Dutch West India Company, managers of the New Amsterdam colony.

Now the oldest house in Queens, the Bowne House reflects the Dutch/ English colonial style in which it was originally built and the vernacular styles it was modified with over the years. Everything here belonged to the Bowne family, making this property a unique documentation of one family's experience in New York practically from the time of its founding to the beginning of the modern era.

In 1694 the Society of Friends moved their meeting out of member John Bowne's house to a newly erected *Quaker Meeting House.* By 1717 the membership had grown so large that the Quakers built an addition onto the Meeting House and doubled the size of the original structure. Since then the house has remained practically unchanged and represents a perfectly preserved early American structure still in use as its builders intended. While the Bowne House is currently undergoing renovations, garden tours can be arranged by calling (718) 359-0528.

The Quaker Meeting House, 137–16 Northern Blvd. (718-358-9636; www .nyym.org), is open for worship every Sunday from 11 a.m. to noon. All are invited to attend. Tours are conducted by appointment, or check the Web site for an updated listing of ongoing open houses.

Skip over the swell of tourists fighting over faux Prada bags and souvenir shops on Canal Street and head to the second largest Chinatown in the city. Flushing, Queens, is home to a fusion of both American and Chinese shops, boutiques, and restaurants. Take the 7 train to Flushing Main Street and walk down Main Street to find the Shi Hong Mall and Golden Shopping Mall for hand pulled noodles, potato and chili salad, and Fujian soup.

Also in Flushing, the *New York State Pavilion* in Flushing Meadows-Corona Park houses a relic of the 1964 World's Fair, only becoming a state landmark in 2009. Here you may recognize one of the largest globes ever made, the Unisphere. Watch out your plane window and see if you can spot it taking off and landing from LaGuardia or JFK. The park's infamous structures include the Queens Theatre in the Park (formerly Theaterama) and restored rocket relics. The park appeared in such movies as *The Wiz* and *Men in Black.*

Get to the pavilion (www.nycgovparks.org) by taking the 7 train to Mets-Willets Point Station, or the E, F, V, or R trains to 71st Avenue and transfer to the Q64 bus.

If you stepped into a gardener's dream and assumed you must have some-how crossed the city boundaries into Long Island, you're still here. *Forest Hills Gardens* is a private and planned 142-acre garden community that was started in 1909 by the Russell Sage Foundation, which was funded by a Wall Street financier's widow. Currently, the Forest Hills Gardens Corporation owns all the streets and sewers (though streets are open to public traffic). While vis-iting the neighborhood, check out Station Square, a Tudor style village center with arch overpasses, red bricks, and medieval style architecture. The square houses a stop for the Long Island Railroad, offering a quick 20-minute com-mute into Manhattan. The *New York Times* called the station one of the most successful public spaces in the city.

The surrounding community is full of 100-plus-year-old homes full of Bavarian flavor and mixed architectural styles. A combination of detached and semi-detached homes lies next to apartment complexes and mansions, all within a small community center. The tallest building is nine stories and was formerly the Forest Hills Inn, which is now a condominium complex. Locals and visitors alike will forget they're still in New York City while walking through the peaceful streets lined with brightly colored gardens.

During your tour, explore the state landmark of the *Church-in-the-Gardens* at 50 Ascan Ave. (718-268-6704; www.thechurchinthegardens .org). The church was founded in 1912 from six different denominations and developed their own community house, sanctuary building, balcony, parish house, and nursery school over the decades.

## For a Little Taste of India

Explore Little India in Jackson Heights, Queens along Seventy-Fourth Street from Roosevelt to 37th Avenue. You can catch a Bollywood feature at the Palace Theater at 73-7 37th Rd. Ladies get pampered at the Gulzar Beauty Salon for traditional henna tattooing and eyebrow threading. Shop for sweets made from paneer, or cottage cheese, at Maharaja Sweets and Snacks at 75-10 37th Ave., or browse for authentic spices and ingredients.

The community of Forest Hills Gardens rests in the Queens neighborhood of Forest Hills, featuring shopping, bars, boutiques, and nightlife along Austin Street and Metropolitan Avenue. Head to *Eddie's Sweet Shop* at 105-29 Metropolitan Ave. for fresh, homemade ice cream. Discover Queens' third largest .park, appropriately named *Forest Hills Park* (www.nycgovparks.org/sub_your_park/vt_forest_park/vt_forest_park.html). The park is shared by a collection of ethnically diverse neighborhoods including Forest Hills, Richmond Hill, Kew Gardens, Woodhaven, and Glendale. The nearly 500-acre park features a historic band shell dating back to 1898, stables, playgrounds, tennis courts, baseball fields, and even a par 67 golf course that is one of the city's most challenging courses. To get to the Forest Hills Park, take the J and Z trains to 85th Street/Forest Parkway, Woodhaven Boulevard, or 105-102 Street stations. You can also take the E and F trains to Union Turnpike.

Have you ever wondered what lies on Queens' eastern shores? Find out with a trek to the *Jamaica Bay Wildlife Refuge Center* nestled on Broad Channel in Queens. It's my favorite spot to get away from the urban grind and remind myself that New York's hidden forests, marshes, and wildlife are all hidden in plain site. Part of the Gateway National Recreation Area, the park is a paradise for nature lovers looking to get away from the city for a few hours. The refuge also holds one of the most diverse groups of inhabitants in the city ranging from salt marshes, upland field and woods, brackish water ponds, and over 330 species of birds. Most impressive to a city dweller, you can see the edges of Manhattan peeking over the water in the far distance. Pass by a few walkers and count how many times you hear, "I can't believe this is New York City!"

The Wildlife Refuge (www.nyharborparks.org) also hosts moonlit walks, bird watching lessons, and special outdoor events. Call (718) 318-4340 for more information. Hike the trails from dawn until dusk seven days a week; the Visitor Contact Station is open from 8:30 a.m. to 5 p.m. daily. By public transportation, take the IND A train to Broad Channel Station.

After exploring the trails at the refuge, take the subway another few stops to *Rockaway Park* (www.nycgovparks.org/parks/Q050/). The Rockaways are often overlooked by visitors and locals alike as a convenient and relaxing beach getaway; they flock to the packed Fire Island, Hamptons, or the Jersey Shore instead. But Far Rockaway was once the premier summer getaway for A-list celebrities- Film alums Mae West and Mary Pickford could be found lounging on the beach. But the heyday of the silent film era wasn't the last time The Rockaways have made it onto a celebrity's radar. Modern day tourists may recognize the area from The Ramones' song, *Rockaway Beach*. Over the years, the neighborhood developed a reputation for crime and elite tourism came to a screeching halt. Eventually it underwent somewhat of a local renaissance and, today, locals head to the Rockaways for an afternoon of Italian ices and walks along the white-sand beaches maintained by the National Park Service.

Hit the local favorite ***Jacob Riis Park*** (www.nyharborparks.org/visit/jari .html), often called "The People's Beach," and wander over to the recently restored Art Deco bathhouse from the 1930s. Today, the architectural landmark houses historical exhibits and ranger-led education programs. The park was built on one of the first U.S. naval air stations and was named for Jacob Riis, a New York City photographer and journalist who documented the turbulent lives of the poor and working class. Visitors can spend the day swimming, playing a round at Putt Golf Course, and trying their luck at Riis Park Pitch. Even on a chilly fall day, locals stroll the beaches and enjoy a break from the crowds of Manhattan.

For more information about Queens attractions, lodging, and things to do, visit www.discoverqueens.info.

## Places to Eat in Queens

**Amici Amore 1**
29–35 Newtown Ave. (30th Street)
(718) 267-2771
www.amiciamore1.com

**Bella Via**
4746 Vernon Blvd.
(48th Avenue)
(718) 361-7510
www.bellaviarestaurant .com

**Caffé on the Green**
201–10 Cross Island Parkway
(718) 423-7272
www.caffeonthegreen.com

**Danny Brown**
10402 Metropolitan Ave.
(718) 261-2144
www.dannybrown winekitchen.com

**Happy Buddha**
135–37 37th Ave.
(718) 358-0079
www.happybuddha.com

**Le Sans Souci**
44–09 Broadway (between 44th and 45th Streets)
(718) 728-2733
www.lesanssouci.net

**Park Side**
107–01 Corona Ave.
(51st Avenue)
(718) 271-9321
www.parksiderestaurant .com

**Piccola Venezia**
42-01 28th Ave.
(718) 721-8470
www.piccola-venezia.com

**Sripraphai**
6413 39th Ave.
(718) 899-9599
www.sripraphairestaurant .com

**Thai Pavilion**
37–10 30th Ave.
(37th Street)
(718) 777-5546

**Tournesol**
5012 Vernon Blvd.
(718) 472-4355
www.tournesolnyc.com

**Trattoria L'incontro**
2176 31st St.
(718) 721-3532
www.trattorialincontro.com

# STATEN ISLAND →

The first recorded European contact with the island was documented during 1524 by Giovanni da Verrazzano who sailed through The Narrows. You may recognize his name from the Verrazzano Bridge, once the longest suspension bridge in the world when it opened in 1964. By 1609, explorer Henry Hudson established Dutch trade in the area and named the island Staten Eylandt after the Staten-General, the Dutch parliament. Staten Island remains the most suburban among its sister boroughs and was officially called the Borough of Richmond until 1975.

Many tourists only notice Staten Island when viewing it from across the water at Battery Park or the Statue of Liberty, sometimes mistaking it for New Jersey. Or they hop on the free ferry for optimum views of Lower Manhattan, wait for the return ride, and never set foot in the borough. But Staten Island has some of the best beaches, historic attractions, and hidden gardens in the city.

Couldn't get a pair of costly tickets to see the New York Yankees? Try the *Staten Island Yankees* instead. Sometimes called The Baby Bombers, the Staten Island Yankees (75 Richmond Terrace; 718-720-9265; www.siyanks.com)

are a class A affiliate of the New York Yankees and play in the New York–Penn League at Richmond County Bank Ballpark along the waterfront in St. George. The stadium is just a short walk from the Staten Island ferry, making it a convenient stop for tourists and locals. Founded in 1999 in a deal brokered by Mayor Rudolph Giuliani, the team was formerly known as the Watertown Indians, an affiliate of the Cleveland Indians. In 2006, the majority owners of the team, the Getzler family, were planning to sell their 51 percent share of the team. The New York Yankees responded by purchasing the Getzler's interest and hired Mandalay Sports Properties to run the day-to-day operations of the team.

There are also plenty of historical attractions to see on Staten Island. While a seventeenth-century Quaker attending a clandestine meeting at the Bowne House might seem to have little in common with a twentieth-century Tibetan Buddhist, the two shared a bond of persecution. One of the uglier aspects of the Maoist period in China was the annexation of Tibet and the suppression of its ancient culture and religion. Despite some recent liberalization on the part of the Chinese occupiers of Tibet, it is still an extremely difficult place to visit; and ironically, those Westerners interested in Tibetan art and religious artifacts have learned to rely on foreign rather than native Tibetan collections. Visit the *Jacques Marchais Museum of Tibetan Art* to see more than a thousand examples of Tibetan religious art—paintings, carved and cast statues, altars, ritual objects, and musical instruments—each of which was created to aid in the meditation that is such an important part of Buddhism, especially as practiced in Tibet.

So who was Jacques Marchais and what is he doing on Staten Island? "He" was a woman named Jacqueline Coblentz Klauber, who operated a Manhattan art gallery under the masculine French pseudonym. Klauber/Marchais had a lifelong interest in things Tibetan, an interest that she said originated in her childhood, when she would play with Tibetan figures her great-grandfather had brought back from the Orient. She never traveled to Tibet, but she carefully added to her collection until her death in 1947.

With its terraced gardens, lily pond, and air of detachment and serenity, the Marchais Museum is a sublime setting for the religious objects that make up the collection, representing centuries of Tibetan culture.

The Jacques Marchais Museum of Tibetan Art, 338 Lighthouse Ave., Staten Island (718-987-3500), is open 1 to 5 p.m. Wednesday through Sunday. Admission is $5 for adults, $3 for senior citizens and students, children under 6 are free. Group tours are also available by appointment. Check www.tibetan museum.org for current exhibits and programs and for information on holiday closings.

Within walking distance of the Marchais Museum lies a Colonial Williamsburg–like living history restoration, complete with a general store, an old county courthouse, and America's oldest elementary school in the area of *Historic Richmond Town.*

Many of its surrounding buildings are staffed by craftspeople working with period equipment and vintage tools. White clapboard farmhouses dot the property's one hundred acres, and a central museum houses exhibits of Staten Island–made products that reveal the history and diversity of New York's least populous borough.

Historic Richmond Town, 441 Clark Ave., Staten Island (718-351-1611; www.historicrichmondtown.org), is open Wednesday through Sunday 1 to 5 p.m. from the day after Labor Day to June 30, with guided tours given at 2:30 p.m. on weekdays and at 2 p.m. and 3:30 p.m. on weekends (visitors must be on tours to enter buildings). From July 1 through Labor Day, hours are Wednesday through Friday 10 a.m. to 5 p.m., and Saturday and Sunday 1 to 5 p.m. During summer, tours are self-guided, with costumed interpreters sharing information along the way. Closed during major holidays; admission is $5 for adults, $4 for seniors, $3.50 for children ages 5 to 17, and free for children under 5. From the Staten Island Ferry, take the S74 bus from the terminal to Richmond Road and St. Patrick's Place.

An authentic *Chinese Scholar's Garden* is just one of the highlights at the inspired eighty-acre Staten Island Botanical Garden on the grounds of Snug Harbor Cultural Center. A meditative display of wood, rocks, water, a variety of plants, and nineteenth-century furniture in the style of the Ming Period are all carefully composed to create an air of quiet meditation. Other displays include a Pond Garden; Heritage Rose, White, and Perennial Gardens; and a Sensory Garden designed to provide physically challenged persons with a garden experience. The garden, at 1000 Richmond Terrace, Staten Island (718-273-8200; www.snug-harbor .org), is open from dawn to dusk. The Chinese Scholar's Garden is open Tuesday through Sunday, 10 a.m. to 5 p.m. Admission to all facilities, including the Newhouse Galleries, is $6 for adults; $5 for seniors and students with I.D.; and $3 for children under 12.

The 260-acre *Clay Pit Ponds State Park Preserve,* New York City's only State Park Preserve, allows visitors to step back in time to a Staten Island of

## staten'ssouth beach

South Beach on Staten Island (718-816-6804), has superb views of the Verrazano-Narrows Bridge; a 7,500-foot-long boardwalk (the fourth largest in the world); and a playground, bocce courts, a roller hockey rink, shuffleboard, ball fields, and picnic areas.

200 years ago. Preserved for its unique geological, botanical, and historical significance, sands and clays were deposited here during the Cretaceous period nearly 70 million years ago. These, along with glacial deposits approximately 12,000 years old, provide a soil that supports a fascinating assemblage of plants such as black jack oaks, American chestnuts, and a variety of ferns in numerous habitats, including ponds, bogs, sandy barrens, freshwater wetlands, and fields. The park is also home to a large number of animals and birds, including raccoons, screech owls, box turtles, and rufous-sided towhees.

During the 1800s, a man named Abraham Ellis and his partner, Balthaser Kreischer, mined clay in this very spot. The men dug it out of a deep, bare pit with shovels and pick axes, and donkeys hauled it on rails to the brickworks to the southwest. The clay was used to make such products as paints, dyes, and laundry bluing. When the mines closed, the pit filled with water and marsh plants thrived. Today, Ellis Swamp is home to cattails and yellow pond lilies, lush vegetation, red-winged blackbirds, spring peepers, and, in early winter, mallard ducks.

The preserve offers a detailed, printed trail guide outlining several walks of varying duration of a half-hour to an hour. Start your hike at the picnic area behind the Park Preserve Headquarters.

***Clay Pit Ponds State Park Preserve,*** 83 Nielsen Avenue, Staten Island (718-967-1976; www.nysparks.com/parks), is open daily from dawn to dusk. Educational programs, including nature walks, pond ecology, bird-watching, and tree and flower identification, are also offered.

***Fort Wadsworth,*** one of the country's oldest military installations, was first used during the American Revolution and was a key component of the New York Harbor defense system until the early 1970s. It became a National Park site and Lighthouse Center and Museum in 1995. Start your visit by viewing the introductory video at the visitor center before heading out on the 1½-mile trail around the site.

The Visitor Center at Fort Wadsworth, Bay Street, Staten Island (718-354-4500), is open Wednesday through Sunday, 10 a.m. to 5 p.m. Call for information on ranger-led tours.

In 1857, while Alexander Graham Bell was a 10-year-old boy living in Scotland, Antonio Meucci developed the first working telephone and transmitted a human voice over a copper wire charged with electricity. While he was busy inventing, he played host to his friend, the great Italian patriot Giuseppe Garibaldi. The globe-trotting Garibaldi, who not only campaigned to drive foreign powers from his beloved Italy but had also fought on behalf of Uruguay in its struggle for independence from Argentina, worked as a candle maker on Staten Island. He was yet to achieve his greatest victory, as the leader of the "red shirts" who liberated Sicily and southern Italy from Bourbon dynastic rule and set the stage for the ultimate defeat of the pope's temporal power and the incorporation of the Papal States into a secular Kingdom of Italy under the House of Savoy.

While it may seem unusual to pay homage to the person the Italians believe was the true inventor of the telephone, you can explore all this and more at the **Garibaldi-Meucci Museum,** 420 Tompkins Ave., Staten Island (718-442-1608; www.garibaldimeucci museum.org). The museum, owned and operated by the Order of the Sons of Italy in America, the oldest organization of Italian-American men and women in the United States and Canada, is open year-round, Tuesday through Sunday 1 to 5 p.m. Admission is $5.

The oldest cultural institution on Staten Island is the **Staten Island Institute of Arts and Sciences** (Staten Island Museum) founded in 1881 and headquartered in the small community of St. George just two blocks from the Staten Island Ferry Terminal. The institute's collection has been accurately described as "eclectic." Exhibits focus on the art, natural science, and cultural history of Staten Island and its people, drawing from the institute's collections of more than two million artifacts and specimens.

## wiseinvestment

In 1810 a 16-year-old Staten Island farm boy named Cornelius Vanderbilt borrowed $100 from his mom to buy a small boat for ferrying passengers and freight across the Narrows to Manhattan. By the time of his death in 1877, "Commodore" Vanderbilt had parlayed that initial investment into a steamship and railroad fortune of $100 million—not bad.

The art collection includes many fine works from ancient to contemporary periods, including works by Staten Island artists such as Jasper Cropsey, Guy Pene du Bois, and Cecil Bell. Also included are pieces by internationally acclaimed talents such as Marc Chagall, Reginald Marsh, and Robert Henri, as well as decorative arts, furniture, clothing, and more. The natural history collections include 500,000 insects, 25,000 plant specimens, and geologic, shell, and archaeological specimens. The archives and library comprise the largest holdings of Staten Island history and science anywhere. Public programs for all ages include weekly "Lunch and Learn" buffets.

The Staten Island Museum, Staten Island Institute of Arts and Sciences, 75 Stuyvesant Place, Staten Island (718-727-1135; www.statenislandmuseum.org), is open Monday through Friday from noon to 5 p.m., Saturday 10 a.m. to 5 p.m., and Sunday noon to 5 p.m. Suggested admission is $2 for adults and $1 for students and senior citizens. Children under 12 are free.

On the south shore of Staten Island is a little-known historical community called **Sandy Ground**—the oldest continuously inhabited free black settlement in the nation. It was founded in the early nineteenth century by freed black men from New York who started a farming community; in mid-century they were joined by free black oyster fishermen from Maryland and Delaware.

Descendents of the original settlers still live on Sandy Ground, and the Sandy Ground Historical Society runs a museum and library that examines the life and history of the freed blacks who settled in the area prior to the Civil War. The museum preserves material related to the historic town, which was a way station on the Underground Railroad. Highlights of the collection include letters, photographs, film, art, rare books, quilts, a letter from W. E. B. DuBois, and other artifacts, such as a can of Tettersalve, a beauty product manufactured by Harlem businesswoman Madame C. J. Walker. *The Sandy Ground Historical Museum* is located at 1538 Woodrow Rd., Staten Island (718-317-5796); admission is $6 for adults and $3 for students and seniors. Spring and summer hours are Tuesday through Thursday and Saturday and Sunday from 1 to 4 p.m.

Clear Comfort, one of the picturesque suburban "cottages" that dotted the shoreline of nineteenth-century Staten Island, was the home of Alice Austen (1866–1952), one of the country's first female photographers. The house was extensively renovated by her father, John, over a period of twenty-five years. By the time he was finished, he had transformed the rundown eighteenth-century Dutch farmhouse into a magnificently landscaped Carpenter Gothic cottage.

Alice lived in the house until illness and financial problems forced her to move in 1945. In the 1960s a group of citizens launched a successful effort to save Clear Comfort, and an exact restoration based on hundreds of Austen's photographs was completed in 1985. The home was designated a New York City Landmark in 1971 and a National Historic Landmark in 1993.

Today the gingerbread-gabled home overlooking the Narrows—the shipping channel for the Port of New York—serves as a gallery for Austen's wonderful photographs documenting life in turn-of-the-twentieth-century America. Changing exhibitions exploring themes inspired by her work and times often use images from the Staten Island Historical Society's Alice Austen Collection of nearly 3,000 negatives. A video narrated by Helen Hayes tells the story of "Alice's World."

*The Alice Austen House,* 2 Hylan Blvd., Staten Island (718-816-4506; www.aliceausten.org/museum), is open Thursday through Sunday from noon to 5 p.m. and closed major holidays and the months of January and February. The grounds are open from dawn until dusk. The museum suggests a donation of $2.

## Fresh Kills

For a truly offbeat attraction, mark your future calendars for a day at *Fresh Kills* (www
.nyc.gov), New York's largest, and perhaps most historic, landfill. Fresh Kills housed
the city's garbage from 1948 to 2001. It also helped process over one million tons
of waste and chemicals after the 9/11 attack on the World Trade Center. According to the Smithsonian National Museum of American History Web site, workers at
Fresh Kills recovered 54,000 personal objects and identified 1,200 victims from the
attack. Currently, an ambitious plan is under way to turn the 2,200 acre landfill into a
world-class park. It will be nearly three times the size of Central Park and showcase
art installations, outdoor markets, nature trails, restaurants, kayaking, and recreation
activities.

Even New York's locals will give a blank stare if you ask about *GANAS* on Staten Island. GANAS, a Spanish word meaning "motivation sufficient to act," houses up to 100 people at any given time. Vegetable gardens flower out amongst the homes and boardwalks connect homes and complexes. Its residents enjoy communal, if not all together experimental, living. Regular house and communal meetings are held and residents learn to live like one big family.

A handful of residents receive a stipend or free room and board in exchange for working in one of the GANAS shops. The Everything Goes shops include a thrift store featuring recycled goods and clothing, a book cafe, furniture, and gallery stores. Anyone can stop by and shop for recycled goods and second-hand items.

Visitors to the GANAS community are welcome by appointment only by calling (718) 720-5368, and are welcome to shop at the Everything Goes store. Check the Web site at www.ganas.org for an updated list of hours of operation. You can get to GANAS from the Staten Island ferry by taking the bus 51 or 76 to Victory Blvd.

# Places to Eat in Staten Island

### Adobe Blues
63 Lafayette Ave.
(718) 720-BLUE
www.silive.com

### Angelina's Restaurant
399 Ellis St.
(718) 227-7100
www.angelinasristorante
.com

### Arirang Hibachi Steakhouse and Sushi Bar
23A Nelson Ave.
(718) 966-9600
www.partyonthegrill.com

### Bayou
1072 Bay St.
(718) 273-4383
www.bayoustatenisland
.com

### Big Nose Kate's Saloon and Eatery
2484 Arthur Kill Rd.
(718) 227-3282

### Brioso Ristorante
174 New Dorp Lane
(718) 667-1700
www.briosoristorante.com

### Caffe Bondi
1816 Hylan Blvd.
(718) 668-0100
www.bondiny.com

### Carol's Café
1571 Richmond Rd.
(718) 979-5600
www.carolscafe.com

### Enoteca Maria
27 Hyatt St.
(718) 447-2777
www.enotecamaria.com

### Fushimi
2110 Richmond Rd.
(718) 980-5300

### Killmeyer's Old Bavaria Inn
4254 Arthur Kill Rd.
(718) 984-1202
www.killmeyers.com

### Parsonage
74 Arthur Kill Rd.
(718) 351-7979

### Yellow Fin
20 Ellis St.
(718) 317-5700

# LONG ISLAND →

Just as New York is simply "The City," Long Island is "The Island," home to hundreds of thousands of commuters taking the LIRR or navigating the tangle of traffic along the congested LIE. Venture out along Route 25A and enter the Great Gatsby era, when the families of fortune—the Vanderbilts, the Chryslers, the Woolworths, the Phippses, the Guggenheims—built astounding mansions sprawling over hundreds of acres, earning this part of the North Shore the nickname the "Gold Coast."

Further east, the magnificent stretch of beach, shopping, and restaurants of the Hamptons call. It's amusing to see how summering Manhattanites who complain about wanting to get away from it all seem to bring it all with them on vacation, then complain even louder than they do in the city about the Hamptons' high summer rents and hectic party atmosphere. For visitors, avoid peak summer months and visit Montauk Point when the weather is blustery, when the wind turns the sea a menacing white-capped green-gray, and empathize for the fishermen and farmers who still make a living from this sea and this land. Long Island's natural beauty has also attracted a number of artists—something about the way light

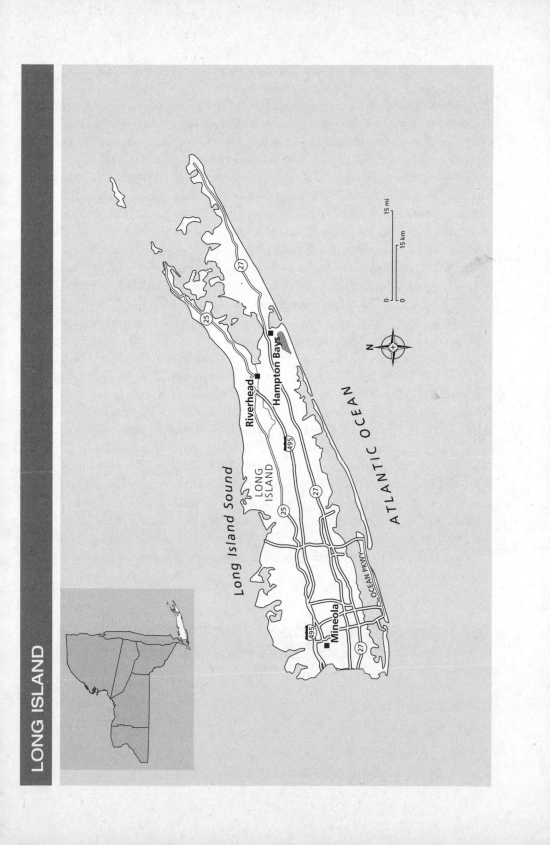

LONG ISLAND

reflects off both the sea and the sound gives the eastern reaches of the island a unique glow.

Howard Gould, son of the railroad baron Jay Gould, spared no expense when he built the 100,000-square-foot mansion *Castlegould* in 1904 on a prime location overlooking the Long Island Sound. See yet another century represented at the 1912 Tudor-style *Hempstead House,* where second owner Daniel Guggenheim resided. In 1923 his son Harry built *Falaise,* a Norman manor filled with period furnishings. Today all three mansions are part of the 216-acre *Sands Point Preserve.*

Castlegould features large traveling natural-history exhibits that change twice a year, plus interactive exhibits changing on a six-month basis. There are six marked nature trails; two of them are self-guiding and one follows the shoreline. In addition to a scattering of geological phenomena, including glacial erratic (large granite boulders dropped from the ice during the last continental glaciations, about 20,000 years ago), there is a wide range of plant and bird life within the preserve. Kids can hit the special Dinosaur Trail, with its replicas of fossilized dinosaur tracks. Pick up trail maps at the visitor center in Castlegould.

Sands Point Preserve is located at 127 Middleneck Rd., Sands Point, Long Island (516-571-7900 or 516-571-7901; www.sandspointpreserve.org). Nature trails are open daily from 10 a.m. to 5 p.m. Admission is $5 per car with a $2 walk-in fee. Falaise is open from early June through late October. Tours run Thursday through Sunday at noon, 1 p.m., 2 p.m., and 3 p.m. from Castlegould; children under 10 are not permitted. Hempstead House is open weekends from early May through late October, 12:30 to 4 p.m.; special natural-history exhibits in Castlegould are $4 for adults, $3 for children and seniors. Both Falaise and the Hempstead House are closed during the September Medieval Festival.

*Planting Fields Arboretum* has just the one sixty-five-room Tudor-style mansion, Coe Hall, former home of insurance magnate William Robertson Coe

## AUTHORS' FAVORITES—LONG ISLAND

Bedell Cellars

Deep Hollow Ranch

Fire Island National Seashore

Montauk Seal Haul-out Trail

Pollock-Krasner House and Study Center

Riverhead Foundation for Marine Research and Preservation

Sagamore Hill

and his wife, Mai Rogers Coe, née Standard Oil heiress. The house and the expansive 409-acre gardens remain much as the wealthy couple coddled them back in the 1920s, with formal gardens, nature trails, and greenhouses filled with William Coe's pet collections, including imported camellias. Coe also set up a working dairy and kept pigs and chickens, donating much of the milk and produce to the needy during the Great Depression.

But it was trees and shrubs that kept Coe's attention preoccupied, and they were the subject of some of his greatest extravagances. The copper beech on the north lawn was moved here from Massachusetts by barge and a team of seventy-five horses when it was already 60 feet high. Working with master landscape gardeners such as A. Robeson Sargent and James Dawson of Olmsted Brothers, Coe created grand *allées* of trees designed to frame the views from the house, and he established rambling azalea walks. As late as the 1950s, in the last years of his life, Coe planted the rhododendron park, which remains one of the outstanding features of Planting Fields.

## motormania

More than two million motor vehicles and nearly 80,000 motor boats are registered in Nassau and Suffolk Counties.

From April through September (except on Labor Day and July 4), visitors can take a self-guided tour of Coe Hall daily noon to 3:30 p.m. There is a $3.50 fee, children 12 and under are free. For tour information call (516) 922-8670. An Upstairs/Downstairs hour-long tour is offered from April 1 to September 30 at 12:30 p.m. and 2:30 p.m.; cost is $3.50 for adults, and children 12 and under are free.

The grounds at Planting Fields Arboretum, 1395 Planting Fields, Oyster Bay, Long Island (516-922-9200; www.plantingfields.org), are open daily 9 a.m. to 5 p.m. There is a $6 entry charge per car daily from May 1 through October and on weekends and holidays the rest of the year. Closed Christmas.

Beyond the Gold Coast lies *The Holocaust Memorial and Educational Center of Nassau County,* on the 204-acre Welwyn Preserve, which hopes to "foster a greater understanding of the causes and consequences of one of the darkest periods in world history." The center hosts ongoing exhibits and has a 1,850-volume library. It's at 100 Crescent Beach Rd. in Glen Cove, Long Island (516-571-8040; www.holocaust-nassau.org), and is open Monday through Friday 9:30 a.m. to 4:30 p.m. and Sunday 11 a.m. to 4 p.m. Admission is free.

If you already saw Teddy Roosevelt's birthplace back in Manhattan, head to his Queen Anne–style pad situated on the rolling grounds of *Sagamore Hill* where he lived from 1885 until his death in 1919. The country's first "Summer White House" features eighty acres of forested terrain, an Old Orchard Museum, and a half-mile loop trail leading down to the pebble strewn banks of sparking Cold Spring Harbor.

Grab a map at the information kiosk and head toward the large windmill just steps from the raised porch wrapping around the Roosevelt home. The inside remains relatively unchanged from its heyday and features flags, paintings, and weapons during Teddy's time on the grounds. Guests can view the drawing room, family bedrooms, nursery, and turn-of-the-century water closet with a porcelain tub. It doesn't take long to see that Teddy knew how to roll. Head back outside and look at your map to locate the former horse stable, a pet cemetery, and tennis courts. The grounds are a peaceful retreat for a relaxing afternoon, though you may stumble upon outdoor concerts, photography exhibits, and horse and carriage demonstrations during summer months.

Head back in the direction of the information kiosk and look for the trail parallel to the parking lot to walk down to *The Roosevelt Museum at Old Orchard.* The museum served as the home of Theodore Roosevelt Jr. and his wife, Eleanor. Apparently they got tired of waiting to inherit the home as promised and decided to build their own home on the grounds. Eleanor was sent away to China for a relaxing trip to escape the chaos of the construction and returned with exotic furnishings for the home. Take a free tour through the living room, dining room, small study, and artifacts from the Roosevelt clan.

My favorite feature of Sagamore Hill isn't the impressive buildings, but Teddy's beloved and well-worn trail leading down to the harbor. You can find the trailhead lurking just behind the Orchard Museum. Bear right and continue down the path until you come to a fork leading to a bridge. Turn right again and walk over the boardwalk down to Cold Spring Harbor, forgetting the Long Island Expressway throbs just a few miles away.

Take a tour of the Roosevelt Home Wednesday through Sunday from 10 a.m. to 4 p.m. on the hour. Admission costs $5 for adults (15 years and older), and free for 15 and under. Arrive early to purchase tickets, as tours are limited to fourteen people and are offered on a first-come, first-served basis. The Roosevelt Museum at Old Orchard is free and open from 10 a.m. to 5 p.m. Sagamore Hill (www.nps.gov/sahi) park grounds are open from dawn to dusk.

Few people still remember whale-oil lamps or whale-bone corsets, but whaling was once an integral and lucrative industry on Long Island, with ships setting out from Sag Harbor and Cold Spring Harbor. Here today the Whaling Museum celebrates the skills and adventures of the town's own whalers as well as those of other men who set out to sea in treacherous conditions from colonial times through the nineteenth century.

*The Whaling Museum* houses a large collection of the implements used in the whale "fishery," as it was known. Here are harpoons, lances, and the tools used in separating blubber from whale carcasses. A permanent exhibit, "Mark Well the Whale," details the history and impact of whaling on the locality. The museum features the state's only fully equipped nineteenth-century whaleboat with original gear; an extensive collection of the whaler's art of scrimshaw; and "The Wonder of Whales" conservation gallery for children.

The Whaling Museum, Main Street, Route 25A, Cold Spring Harbor, Long Island (631-367-3418; www.cshwhalingmuseum.org), is located off of Route 25A and is open daily from Memorial Day through Labor Day; closed Monday the rest of the year. Hours are 11 a.m. to 5 p.m. Admission is $6 for adults $5 for seniors and students 5 to 18; families (parents and children) pay $19.

*The DNA Learning Center,* the educational arm of Cold Spring Harbor Laboratory, is the world's first biotechnology museum completely devoted to genetics education. Two- and three-dimensional displays, computer multimedia, videos, and other elements are utilized to teach visitors about genes in a presentation called "The Genes We Share," free Monday through Friday 10 a.m. to 4 p.m. and Saturday noon to 4 p.m.

The DNA Learning Center is located at 334 Main St., Cold Spring Harbor, Long Island (516-367-5170; www.dnalc.org); admission is free.

Be sure to stop by National Landmark *St. James General Store* at 516 Moriches Rd., St. James (631-854-3740; www.suffolkcounty.gov). In business since 1857, it's the oldest continuously operating general store in the country and looks just as it did in 1890. The shelves are stocked with more than 4,000 items, many of which are nineteenth-century reproductions, including handmade quilts, salt-glaze pottery, hand-carved decoys, penny candy, exotic teas, and bonnets. The store is open daily except Monday from 10 a.m. to 5 p.m.

The village of *Stony Brook* on Long Island Sound boasts a scenic location, a fascinating history, great food and lodgings, museums, and varied shopping. And it owes its present-day success primarily to the vision of Ward Melville who helped the rural village to successfully transform into a suburban center while still retaining its historic integrity. His plan, unveiled to the community in 1939, called for relocating businesses and homes to open the view to the harbor. The shops were moved to

## suburbansprawl

Levittown, the country's first instant suburb, was created in 1947 when 17,400 freestanding houses were erected.

a "shopping center" at the head of the village green, and today more than forty of the trendiest shops on Long Island are housed at the Stony Brook Village

Center. Up the road the Three Village Garden Club Exchange features two floors of antiques and collectibles.

Built in 1751, Stony Brook's *Three Village Inn* was until 1867 the home of Captain Jonas Smith, Long Island's first millionaire sea captain. Today it's a charming inn and restaurant, a winner of the *Wine Spectator* Award of Excellence. It features homemade breads and desserts and house specialties such as cold plum soup, pan-roasted chicken breast stuffed with ham and Monterey Jack cheese, baked lobster pie, and, every Sunday, a "Thanksgiving" turkey dinner with all the trimmings. The inn is located at 150 Main St., Stony Brook, Long Island (www.threevillageinn.com). To make a room or meal reservation (breakfast, lunch, dinner, and Sunday brunch), call (516) 751-0555.

Within walking distance of the inn, at 1200 Route 25A, is the *Long Island Museum of American Art, History and Carriages.* This museum complex houses the *Margaret Melville Blackwell History Museum,* featuring American decor in miniature in a gallery of fifteen period rooms and one of the country's finest collections of antique decoys, plus a new exhibition, every two or three months, on a historical theme; the *Dorothy and Ward Melville Carriage House,* with its world-renowned collection of more than ninety horse-drawn carriages; and the *Art Museum,* exhibiting American art from the eighteenth century to the present, as well as collected works of American genre painter William Sidney Mount (1807–68). There are also a 1794 barn, an 1867 carriage shed, an 1875 blacksmith shop, an 1877 one-room schoolhouse, and a colonial burying ground. The museums are open daily in July and August; the rest of the year they're open Wednesday through Saturday 10 a.m. to 5 p.m. and Sunday noon to 5 p.m. Closed Monday (except Monday holidays) and Tuesday. Also closed New Year's, Thanksgiving, Christmas Eve, and Christmas Day. Admission is $9 for adults, $7 for seniors, $4 ages 6 to 17, $4 for college students with ID; under 6 free. Admission covers everything on the 9-acre grounds. For information call (631) 751-0066 or visit www.longislandmuseum.org.

longisland**trivia**

The largest island adjoining the continental United States, Long Island is approximately 118 miles long and 20 miles at its widest. Long Island has more than 150 beaches; the largest is 2,400-acre Jones Beach. King Kullen, the country's first supermarket, opened on Long Island in 1930.

Don't leave town before seeing the still working *Stony Brook Gristmill* on Harbor Road, built during 1751. The mill was acquired by and renovated through the efforts of philanthropist Ward Melville in 1947 and is currently Long Island's most fully equipped working gristmill.

The mill is open in May and June and September through December on weekends noon to 4:30 p.m.; in July and August it's open Friday, Saturday, and Sunday noon to 4:30 p.m. Admission is $2 for adults and $1 for children under 12. For information call (631) 751-2244. The Ward Melville Heritage Association, which operates the mill, also offers Discovery Wetlands Cruises; call (631) 751-2244 for information and ticket prices, or reserve online at www .wmho.org.

## Central Nassau, the South Shore, then Heading East

In Nassau County, the city of **Hempstead** is home to the **African American Museum,** founded in 1970 as the Black History Exhibit Center. In addition to local lore and history of slaves and free blacks, who worked at farming, whaling, crafts, and small businesses, the museum includes interpretive exhibits of traditional and contemporary native African culture.

The African American Museum tells the story of Long Island's blacks through displays of photographs, artifacts, lectures, workshops, and performing arts. Local artistic talent is especially promoted. African-oriented exhibits and special programs have included shows devoted to West African crafts, art from Sierra Leone, African toys, and black artistic expression in South Africa.

**The African American Museum** (110 North Franklin St., Hempstead, Long Island; 516-572-0730; www.aamoflongisland.org) is open Tuesday through Saturday 10 a.m. to 5 p.m.; admission is free.

Head to the nearby Rock Hall Museum, a 1767 mansion built by Tory merchant Josiah Martin. Rock Hall represents the high-water mark of late Georgian architecture in this part of the country, particularly in its interior detailing. The paneling and mantels, as well as much of the eighteenth- and early nineteenth-century furniture and the replica of a colonial kitchen (the original kitchen was in an outbuilding), came down practically unchanged to our own time. Josiah Martin's family, having come through the revolution none the worse for being on the wrong side, lived here until 1823. The following year Thomas Hewlett bought Rock Hall; his family lived in the mansion for more than a century after his death in 1841. In 1948

## soundsfishytome

The first pastor of East Hampton's "Old Church" (built in 1717) received a salary of "forty-five pounds annually, lands rate free, grain to be first ground at the mill every Monday and one-fourth of the whales stranded on the beach."

## ANNUAL EVENTS ON LONG ISLAND

**JANUARY**

**Long Island Winterfest**
www.liwinterfest.org
(through March)

**FEBRUARY**

**Long Island Boat Show**
Uniondale
(631) 691-7050
www.NYMTA.com

**MARCH**

**Hamptons Restaurant Week**
www.hamptonsrestaurantweek.com

**Saint Patrick's Day Parade**
Montauk
(631) 668-1578
www.montaukfriendsoferin.com

**Shakespeare Festival**
Hofstra University
(516) 463-6644

**MAY**

**Dutch Festival**
Hofstra University
(516) 463-6582

**Long Island Lighthouse Challenge**
Various locations
(631) 207-4331
www.LilighthouseSociety.org

**JUNE**

**Belmont Stakes**
Elmont
(516) 488-6000

**JULY**

**July 4th at Jones Beach**
Wantagh
(631) 669-1000

**Mercedes-Benz Polo Challenge**
Bridgehampton
(212) 421-1367
www.sportpolo.com

**AUGUST**

**Hampton Classic Horse Show**
Bridgehampton
(631) 537-3177
www.hamptonclassic.com

---

the Hewletts gave the place to the town of Hempstead—presumably then a larger municipal entity—for use as a museum.

*Rock Hall Museum* (199 Broadway, Lawrence, Long Island; 516-239-1157; www.toh.li) is open year-round, Wednesday through Saturday 10 a.m. to 4 p.m. and Sunday noon to 4 p.m. Admission is free.

With eight-and-a-half miles of waterfront, *Freeport* calls itself "the Boating and Fishing Capital of the East." Woodcleft Avenue, informally known as *Nautical Mile,* is rumored to once have been a haven for bootleggers, pirates, and other scoundrels. Today it is a mecca for sightseers, browsers, and seafood lovers. Restaurants, pubs, fish markets, and gift shops line the avenue, and one of the island's largest charter/sport fishing fleets sails out of the harbor daily in season.

**Hamptons Wine and Food Festival**
East Hampton
(631) 613-3110
www.hamptonswineandfood.com

**SEPTEMBER**

**Sag Harborfest**
Sag Harbor
(631) 725-1700

**Shinnecock Pow-Wow**
Shinnecock Reservation
(631) 283-6143
www.shinnecocknation.com

**OCTOBER**

**Hamptons International Film Festival**
East Hampton and other locations
(631) 324-4600
www.hamptonsfilmfest.org

**Long Island Halloween**
Old Bethpage Village
(516) 572-8400
www.oldbethpage.org

**The Oyster Festival**
Oyster Bay
(516) 628-1625
www.theoysterfestival.org

**NOVEMBER**

**Long Island Festival of Trees**
Uniondale
(516) 378-2000
www.ucpn.org

**Thanksgiving Antique Show**
Old Westbury
(516) 868-2751

**Thanksgiving Celebration**
Old Bethpage
(516) 572-8400
www.oldbethpage.org

**DECEMBER**

**Charles Dickens Festival**
Port Jefferson
(631) 473-5220

**Holiday Lights Spectacular**
Wantagh
(516) 221-1000

Though Long Island may be better known for its strips of mega-malls, you can still find independent shops like *Dear Little Dollies.* More than 6,000 dolls spill out of every nook and cranny of the 5,000-square-foot store. Sure, you can find Barbie hanging out here with Ken and the gang, but also one-of-a-kind dolls and limited editions by contemporary artists such as Yolanda Bello and Paul Crees; ethnic dolls; and mid-priced dolls from makers including Seymour Mann and Ashton-Drake Galleries. Prices range from $20 to $14,000. Dorothy and Louis Camilleri, owners of Dear Little Dollies, host numerous artist signings in the shop and special shows in the gallery. They also offer a mail-order service; call or check the store's Web site at www.dldollies.com for details. Dear Little Dollies (418 Bedford Ave., Bellmore, Long Island; 516-679-0164) is open Monday through Saturday 10 a.m. to 6 p.m. and Sunday from noon until 5 p.m.

Not far from Bellmore is the **Bide-a-Wee Pet Cemetery** in Wantagh, where Richard Nixon's beloved cocker spaniel, Checkers, rests in peace. Checkers died in 1964 and was buried in plot #5. He is now surrounded by about 50,000 other deceased companion animals. The cemetery is on Beltagh Avenue opposite Wantagh High School.

On Long Island's south shore in **Seaford,** the **Tackapausha Museum and Preserve** is an eighty-acre introduction to the ecology and natural history of the Northeast's coastal woodlands. Tackapausha is named after a *sachem* (or chief) of Long Island's Massapequas, who once lived on this land without greatly affecting its wildlife, its plant communities, or the balance of natural forces.

## longisland ferryservice

Two companies offer year-round ferry service across the Long Island Sound to and from Connecticut. Cross Sound Ferry, Inc. (631-323-2525 or 860-443-5281) operates between New London and Orient Point; Bridgeport and Port Jefferson Ferry Co. (631-473-0286 or 888-44-FERRY) runs between Bridgeport and Port Jefferson. Both rides take approximately seventy-five minutes each way.

The Tackapausha Museum is a small facility designed to serve as an introduction to the plants and animal life of the preserve itself. Exhibits explain the relationship between habitat groups, the differences between diurnal and nocturnal animals, and the changes in life patterns brought about by the different seasons. There is also a small collection of native animals, housed in as natural a setting as possible. The preserve itself is a lovely piece of land, incorporating a variety of ecosystems. A self-guiding trail takes visitors through the different environments; you can pick up the interpretive map at the museum.

The Tackapausha Museum and Preserve (Washington Avenue, Seaford, Long Island; 516-571-7443) is open Tuesday through Saturday 10 a.m. to 4 p.m. and Sunday 1 to 4 p.m. Admission is $3 for adults, $2 for children ages 5 to 14, and free for those under 5.

I thought I had stumbled back to my roots in the South, but no, it's just Old Bethpage Village Restoration, a re-creation of a Long Island village of the Civil War era, long before there was ever a Levittown or Long Island Expressway. Or a celebrity hold on the Hamptons. During the 1960s, the officials began moving threatened colonial and early-nineteenth-century structures to the restoration area. There are now nearly fifty buildings on the site, representing the typical domestic, commercial, and agricultural structures of the time.

The guides at Old Bethpage Village wear historical attire and its skilled craftspeople and a local militia roam the grounds. Civil War re-enactments are common with performances by the re-created Company "E" of the 14th Brooklyn Regiment. (Talk about an inner turmoil of allegiance—do I side with my Southern roots from Georgia, where some people still call it "The War Between the States," or pay homage to the borough I call home?) *Old Bethpage Village Restoration,* 1303 Round Swamp Rd. (exit 48 off the LIE), Old Bethpage (516-572-8400; www.oldbethpage.org), is open Wednesday through Friday 10 a.m. to 4 p.m. and Saturday and Sunday 10 a.m. to 5 p.m. in summer and early fall. Call for other openings. Closed holidays except Memorial Day, July 4, Labor Day, and Columbus Day, when the restoration is closed the day after each of these days. Admission is $10 for adults and $7 for children 5 to 12, senior citizens, and volunteer firefighters (ticket sales end one hour before closing). Call for information on special presentations and events.

Ever wanted to walk in the footsteps of Walt Whitman? You can with a visit to his birthplace and a stroll through a wooded forest to Jayne's Hill. Whitman was born in 1819 in a West Hills farmhouse his father had built nine years earlier. I was surprised to learn suburban encroachment almost swallowed the historic home, and it wasn't until 2001 that it was meticulously restored, though the area surrounding the home is full of malls, fast-food chains, and rambling trucks. It's currently the only New York State Historic Site on Long Island listed on the National Register of Historic Places.

While the home is a charming escape from suburban Long Island complete with an Interactive Center and insight into Whitman's life, I prefer to walk in the great poet's footsteps to Jayne's Hill in West Hills County Park. Grab a map and make the loop hike from his birthplace to the highest point in Long Island. Jayne's Hill rests nearly 400 feet above sea level and is said to be one of Walt Whitman's most beloved spots. It's easy to see why he wrote "The high hill affords an extensive and pleasant view." Poetry lovers and secret writers can't help but stand still beside the rock and plaque marking the hill and wait, hoping to capture some of Whitman's inspiration.

The *Walt Whitman Birthplace* is located at 246 Old Walt Whitman Rd. Visit www.waltwhitman.org or call (631) 427-5240 for more information and directions.

Long Island is fit for a king, at least an Albanian president who decreed himself king and lived a rather eccentric and paranoid lifestyle in East Norwich. Legends and rumors have always festered around *Muttontown Preserve* and the Knollwood estate, a sixty-room granite palace built in the 1900s by Charles Hudson that has long since crumbled. The mansion was known as one of the elite homes along Long Island's Gold Coast. It caught the attention of Ahmed Bey Zogu in 1951 and he promptly purchased the estate. He was the president of Albania from 1925 to 1928 before deciding he wanted to be the king instead, and was henceforth known as King Zog I. He allegedly paid around $100,000 in rubies and diamonds, prompting treasure hunters to later vandalize the grounds to search for loot they believe he buried. Considering how paranoid Zog sounded (reclusive, persistent fear of being assassinated, made his Mom work in the royal kitchen to make sure his food wasn't being poisoned), I'm tempted to grab a shovel myself.

While the impressive estate has long since fallen into disrepair and was mostly destroyed, you can still see some of its remains. Walk behind the Visitor Center and take a map before venturing to the trail on your left to make your way out to the ruins. I strongly discourage, if not outright forbid, anyone from hiking this area alone. Even with a map, GPS, and knowledge of the area, I still got turned around and lost on more than one occasion on the tangle of trails and secluded woods.

By the time you make your way down to Zog's ruins, you'll be so accustomed to the thick forest cover housing peeking rhododendron and wineberry, that seeing Zog's crumbling mansion tucked deeply into the woods will give you a start. Consider that the site was once home to a stone mansion with balustrades and grandiose columns, now resembling Roman ruins complete with a decaying fountain. As you make your way up its ominous steps, you'll come to terms with the fact that these woods are probably haunted. Shadowy trees and twisted trails lead through overgrown weeds and marshy outcroppings. Nearby, there's also a garden wall and trails winding through the preserve, in all some 550 acres of fields, woodlands, and ponds.

If you're looking for a well-preserved piece of Long Island's Gold Coast on Muttontown Preserve, check out the 40-room **Chelsea Mansion** built by Benjamin Moore and his wife in 1924. Moore was the first mayor of Muttontown Village, and his great-great-grandfather, Clement Clark Moore, penned *A Visit from St. Nicholas*—you might know it better as *'Twas the Night Before Christmas*. (And if you've already read though the Manhattan section of this guidebook, you'll remember Clement is buried in Manhattan's only active cemetery, Trinity Cemetery, at 155th Street.) The exquisite Chelsea Mansion is complete with a courtyard moat and bridge, the French Normandy–style mansion blends English and Chinese influences thanks to Mrs. Moore's affinity for Asian décor after a honeymoon in China. The home somehow manages to look both exotic and refined. The mansion is intermittently open for tours during the year for $12 for adults, $8 for seniors, and $5 for children ages 8 to 17. Call (516) 571-8551 in advance for an updated schedule.

Buried in 1,750 acres at Caumsett State Historic Park is the former home of Marshal Field III, the grandson of the department-store magnate. Field bought the property in 1921 and named it after the Indian word meaning "place by a sharp rock." He worked to turn it into a world-class hunting preserve and country club offering just about every sport imaginable, except golf. The grounds were designed to be self-sustaining and relied on its own cattle, a garden, water supply, and power lines. In the early 1960s the state of New York turned it into a public park for fishing, horseback riding, hiking, guided walks, fishing, scuba diving, nature programs, and recreation. Visitors can park and explore the working dairy complex, riding stables, walled gardens, or hike through its trails. Start with a walk along the main road and cruise past the Winter Cottage, a home that would make Long Island's elite flush with envy.

I personally enjoy the hike out past the fishing pond and to the rocky shores of Long Island Sound. I somehow feel I've stumbled outside the park and into a secluded area meant only for me. I guess now I'll have to share my special spot. The last time I was there, a rope swing hung from the elbow of a large, knotted tree just off the sandy path. Hop on and watch the water roll over the pebble strewn shoreline below.

*Caumsett State Historic Park* is located at 25 Lloyd Harbor Rd. in Huntington and is open year-round from sunrise to sunset, with a $6 per car admission fee from April through November. Visit nysparks.state.ny.us/parks/23/details.aspx for more information.

Over in Centerport, more than 40 acres house the sprawling mansion of William Kissam Vanderbilt II, the great-grandson of Commodore Cornelius. The Vanderbilts were never known for being modest, and built their home for optimal views of the Northport Harbor and Long Island Sound. The grounds blend an eccentric look at a Gold Coast–era mansion, boathouse, planetarium, fine arts exhibits, marine museum, photographs, and a seaplane hangar. One of the exhibits was open to the public during William Vanderbilt's heyday, "The Hall of Fish." What else could they do with the grounds but turn it into a museum and learning center? Don't leave without checking out a 238-seat planetarium with three different shows on weekends and holidays, and a domed, 60-foot Sky Theater with a GOTO star projector that can show 11,369 stars on a clear night.

The *Vanderbilt Museum* (631-854-5555; www.vanderbiltmuseum.org) is located at 180 Little Neck Rd. in Centerport. The grounds, mansion, and historic exhibits are open Tuesday through Friday noon to 5 p.m., Saturday 11 a.m. to 5 p.m., and Sunday noon to 5 p.m. Visit the plantarium on Friday night from 8 to 10 p.m., on Saturday from 11 a.m. to 10 p.m., and Sunday from noon to 4 p.m.

There are many options available on the grounds, so consider a general admission ticket and spend the better part of a day. General admission runs $7 for adults, $6 for seniors 62 and older and students with ID, and $3 for children under 12. The fee includes freedom to roam the estate grounds, the Marine Museum, Mansion Memorial, Nursey Wing with video tour and a view of an Egyptian mummy, dinosaur exhibit, and dioramas. You can choose to pay $5 per ticket for a planetarium show. There is another 50 cent charge in evenings for children under 12 and an evening laser show runs $10 adults, $9 student and seniors, and $8 for children under 12.

Like Planting Fields in Oyster Bay, the south shore's ***Bayard-Cutting Arboretum State Park*** is another rich man's estate whose gracious gardens and majestic trees can now be enjoyed by all. William Bayard Cutting (1850–1912) was one of New York City's ablest financiers, as well as a lawyer, railroad director and president, insurance executive, and a philanthropist noted for having built the first block of Manhattan tenements to feature indoor plumbing.

In his leisure time (whenever that might have been), Cutting enjoyed tinkering with his scenic Long Island retreat, located near present-day ***Connetquot River State Park Preserve.*** Cutting did not believe in skimping, and when he built his sixty-eight-room Tudor mansion in 1886, he asked his friend Louis Comfort Tiffany to add a few decorative touches. When it came to landscaping, Cutting placed a great deal of trust in another friend, the great Harvard botanist and silviculturist Charles Sprague Sargent. Working with landscape architect Frederick Law Olmsted, who laid out Central Park, Sargent beautified the estate with flowering azaleas and rhododendrons along footbridges and stream banks.

***The Bayard-Cutting Arboretum State Park*** (Route 27A, Great River, Long Island; 631-581-1002; www.bayardcuttingarboretum.com) is open Tuesday through Sunday 10 a.m. to sunset, as well as holiday Mondays between April and October. Admission is $6 per car; free from November through April 3. Tours of the mansion are available on Sunday at 2 p.m. for an additional $6 donation. Special holiday tours are also available. Seasonally, art exhibits and Sunday series include baroque violin and piano concerts. Call the park in advance for an updated schedule.

Within a few miles of the Bayard-Cutting Arboretum are the village of West Sayville and the ***Long Island Maritime Museum.*** The whalers of Cold Spring Harbor weren't the only brave Long Islanders to battle the sea to pursue their quarry; in West Sayville, men went out into treacherous waters to harvest the coveted oyster. The maritime museum includes a restored vintage 1907 oyster house and showcases the largest collection of small craft on Long Island. There is also a restored boat-builder's shop, illustrative of the skill and care that went into the building of these essential commercial vessels. Other exhibits focus on the tools of oystermen over the years.

# Fire Island Ferry Service

There are no cars allowed on Fire Island. The ferry is the only way to reach its seventeen communities. Sunken Forest Ferry Service (631-589-0810) departs Sayville for Sunken Forest from May to October; Sayville Ferry Service (631-589-0810) services Fire Island Pines and Cherry Grove, April to November; Davis Ferry Co. (631-475-1665) goes from Patchogue to Davis Park, Watch Hill, and Fire Island Seashore from March to September; Fire Island Ferries (631-665-3600) leaves from Bay Shore for Saltaire, Ocean Beach, Atlantique, Kismet, Dunewood, Fair Harbor, Seaview, and Ocean Bay Park year-round.

Along with oysters, find displays of yachting and racing memorabilia, model boats, and artifacts related to the lifesaving service of the nineteenth century round out the museum's collection. Duck and other shorebird decoys, an integral part of American folk art in shoreline communities well into the twentieth century, are also on exhibit. The Bayman's Cottage depicts the style of living at the turn of the twentieth century.

Long Island Maritime Museum (86 West Ave. [Route 27A], West Sayville, Long Island; 631–HIS–TORY; www.limaritime.org) is open Monday through Saturday 10 a.m. to 4 p.m. and Sunday noon to 4 p.m. Admission is $4 for adults, and $2 for seniors and children.

A narrow barrier island off Long Island's southern shore, Fire Island is a popular gay getaway with lots of partying, though plenty of families also summer here far more quietly and modestly. *Fire Island National Seashore* stretches for 32 miles from *Robert Moses State Park* in the west to *Smith Point Park* in the east. Though both parks are accessible by car, the towns sandwiched in between can be reached only by boat or on foot. Designated a "forever preserved wilderness area," the seashore is home to herons, wild geese, and deer (be alert for deer ticks, carriers of Lyme disease, when you're in high grass). Among the must-see spots is the *Sunken Forest* at Sailors Haven, one of the last maritime forests remaining on the eastern seaboard. The forest houses 40 acres of twisted, knotted trees shaped by salt spray and a freshwater marshland. Boardwalks, sand dunes, and 200-year-old trees house a diversity of wildlife, making it a favorite for bird watchers.

Although situated more closely on the beaten tourist path, I still have a soft spot for the boardwalk stroll out to the *Fire Island Lighthouse.* While many think of the Statue of Liberty as an iconic greeting to freedom and immigration, the Fire Island Lighthouse was an immigrant's first glimpse at New York when arriving from Europe. Previously, a 74-foot-high, octagonal lighthouse was erected in 1826 and proved ineffective due to its short stature. It was eventually removed and, in 1858, the new lighthouse was lit on November 1. It was eventually decommissioned in 1973. Over the years, the iconic structure was neglected before the Fire Island Lighthouse Preservation Society banded together in the early 1980s and managed to secure a starring spot for the lighthouse on the National Register of Historic Places and re-commissioned the lighthouse in 1986.

From the parking lot, follow along the boardwalk leading up to the light-house. I prefer to take this route, and then return with a jaunt down the shore-line. Don't be surprised if you see deer hanging out directly next to the walk, scrounging on weeds and giving a hopeful eye to tourists with a snack in hand. Deer control is a major problem on Fire Island. Please respect the posted rules and don't be tempted to pet or feed them. Once you reach the lighthouse, take a tour of the inside to see views over the expanse of Fire Island. Or you can peruse the adjacent museum for free.

Fire Island Lighthouse (east of Robert Moses State Park; 631-661-4876; www.fireislandlighthouse.com), operates daily tours from April through June from 9:30 a.m. to 5 p.m., and July 1 to Labor Day from 9:30 a.m. to 6 p.m. Visit from Labor Day to mid-December from 9:30 a.m. to 5 p.m. On weekends from mid-December to March, the lighthouse is open from noon to 4 p.m. and weekdays 10 a.m. to 4 p.m. Tower tours cost $6 for adults, $4 for seniors 65 and older, children, and active duty military personnel with IDs. Children must be at least 42" tall to climb the tower. For information, contact the National Parks Service at (631) 289-4810 or www.nps.gov.

Remains of Long Island's Gold Coast, a forgotten tavern, a trout hatchery, an old gristmill, multiple bird sanctuaries, and hidden trails all sprawl across **Connetquot River State Park Preserve.** The park spans some 3,473 acres of land and water and once attracted a group of wealthy sportsmen to its private trout stream and ample hunting opportunities. The Main House, just a bit up the road off the park entrance, was once an 1800s watering hole called Snedecor's Tavern and catered to Long Island's elite and blue bloods. There's a suggestion that the owner, Eliphalet "Liff" Snedecor, started the insurgence of Gold Coast settlers with his good food and brews.

## ontheair

In 1901 Guglielmo Marconi sent his first radio transmission from Fire Island Avenue in Babylon.

Turn right at the gristmill and then left again at the first footpath, with a park map handy, to make your way through the winding trails to the trout hatchery. It's not unusual to see deer walk right up the trail, curiously eyeing hikers while waterfowl and rare nesting osprey call nearby. When you get to the 144-year-old hatchery, take a moment to explore and learn about the life cycle of the trout. Though it has recently been plagued by a river virus and closed indefinitely for eradication, you can still read the signs and learn about its history.

A free permit must be obtained in writing or at the park entrance upon arrival and there is a $6 per vehicle fee. More information and directions can be found at nysparks.state.ny.us/parks/8/details.aspx.

Elsie Collins's *1880 House* is an antiques-filled bed-and-breakfast just a few blocks from Westhampton Beach. There are two large suites in the farmhouse, each with its own adjoining sitting room and private bath, and a third in an adjacent one-hundred-year-old barn. Guests cool off in the swimming pool after a game of tennis or warm up by the fireplace after a brisk winter's walk along the beach. The B&B, at 2 Seafield Lane, Westhampton Beach, Long Island (631-288-1559 or 800-346-3290), is open year-round.

If you've always wanted to sleep in the same bed as Jack Nicholson—don't we all?—we've got a great place for you: the Southampton Inn. (Columbia Films rented the entire inn during the 2003 filming of *Something's Gotta Give*.) This hostelry is truly pet (and family) friendly and allows your furry companions to eat breakfast with you right in the library. But don't expect to see piles of chew toys and furniture covered in a fresh coat of dog hair. The ninety-room Tudor-style hotel offers elegant accommodations, fine dining, conference facilities, a heated swimming pool, all-weather tennis, a fitness room, a game room, and beach access. If you're not a pet person, ten Romance Rooms (off-limits to pets, kids, and smoking) have been set aside in a separate building.

*The Southampton Inn* (91 Hill St., Southampton, Long Island; 800-832-6500; www.southamptoninn.com) is open year-round.

In 1954 abstract expressionist painter Jackson Pollock moved with his wife, artist Lee Krasner, to a two-story 1879 shingled house overlooking Accabonac Creek. He lived here until his death in 1956, painting some of his most famous pieces in the studio he converted from a barn.

Today at the Pollock-Krasner House and Study Center, visitors can tour the artists' studio and their home, filled with the couple's furniture and belongings, and their library, including Pollock's extensive collection of jazz albums. Also on view is a documentary photo essay chronicling Pollock's artistic development and detailing his working methods.

The Study Center, established to promote scholarship in twentieth-century American art, houses a growing art reference library built around the personal papers of those who witnessed the birth of abstract expressionism.

## Not Where, But When

The streets in the Hamptons may see as much Manolo-shod foot traffic as anyplace on the French Riviera; for travelers seeking the serenity these seaside villages once offered, avoid the summer season. In spring and fall, prices, crowds, and traffic are all far gentler and the weather? Sublime.

*The Pollock-Krasner House and Study Center* (830 Fireplace Rd., East Hampton; 631-324-4929) is open May through October from Thursday to Saturday. One-hour guided tours are available in May, September, and October from 11 a.m. to 4 p.m., and in June, July, and August at 1 to 5 p.m.; call for appointments the rest of the year. Tours are given every hour on the hour. Admission is $5 adults (guided tours $10 with advance reservations), kids under 12 free. State and city university students, faculty, and staff are also admitted free.

Every now and then a whale, dolphin, or seal turns up on the shores in New York, especially Long Island. (Though it's not unheard of for a stray seal to end up in the Gowanus Canal in Brooklyn.) The Riverhead Foundation for Marine Research and Preservation rescues any whale, porpoise, dolphin, seal, or sea turtle stranded anywhere in New York. Established in 1980, the organization has handled more than 2,000 strandings, including the first and only successful rehabilitation and release of a baby sperm whale.

The Visitor Center briefs people on what to do if they find a stranded creature. On their list of do's and don'ts: don't attempt to push the animal back into the water or obstruct the blowhole; do notify the foundation and keep crowds away. It also has exhibits on sea turtles, harbor seals (when available), and other sea life.

*Riverhead Foundation for Marine Research and Preservation's Visitor Center* (467 East Main St., Riverhead, Long Island; 631-369-9840; www .riverheadfoundation.org) is open from 10 a.m. to 5 p.m. daily July through Labor Day, and weekends only the rest of the year. Admission is $4 for adults and $2 for children. The foundation also operates seal-watching cruises and seal walks; call for details.

During my tenure writing family travel pieces, it's come to my attention that there are just as many adults as children who are obsessed with trains. Toy trains, real trains, Thomas the train, vintage trains, cartoon trains, and anything with wheels on tracks. When my young nephews Sam and Jack are old enough to head to New York, they'll probably somehow sense there is a *Railroad Museum of Long Island* in Riverhead waiting for them. Guests can peruse a collection of trains ranging from steam engine #39, diesel engine #1556, porter engine #1, a variety of vintage cars, and the first Long Island Railroad all-aluminum, double-decker passenger car—I wish they still had that variety running out of Penn Station. But kids will probably be more interested in the miniature railroad than the indoor museum. The admission price includes a whirl on a World's Fair miniature train and guided tour.

The Riverhead site is located at 416 Griffin Ave. north of the railroad tracks and is open from 10 a.m. to 4 p.m. Admission runs $5 for adults 13 years and older and $3 for children 5 to 12 years old, children 5 and under are free. There is also another site in Greenport with hours from 11 a.m. to 4 p.m. Bring your ticket from the Riverhead site and enter for free on the same day you purchased a ticket. Visit www.rmli.us/RMLI for more information.

If trains don't blow your whistle, try the *Atlantis Marine World Aquarium* in Riverhead. The aquarium takes on a "Lost City of Atlantis" theme with indoor exhibits and outdoor learning along the Petonic River. The decor is a bit garish at times, with a cutout of Atlantis lording over the building, oversized sea train, and murals of the sea. Inside, you won't care about the decor and will be distracting yourself with the touch tank full of stingray. Despite their name, the stingrays are friendly enough to pet and feed. You can also handle bugs, including the loudly annoying Madagascar hissing cockroaches, snakes, a bearded dragon reptile, and spiders. The squeamish can watch the penguins, alligators, and a sea lion show from afar or check out the Interactive Salt Marsh. Ask the staff about snorkling right in the reef for an additional fee.

What I appreciate about the aquarium is that it offers you the opportunity to get outside and explore nature for yourself. Guests can take an Atlantis Explorer Tour Boat for a ride down the Peconic and into Flanders Bay with a stop at Hubbard County Park for exploration. On the way, on-board educators pass around star fish and other creatures to touch and examine. There's also an Interactive Salt Marsh exhibit alongside the Peconic River for a look at a typical marine habitat. I wasn't really sure what they were for, but apparently they help remove toxins and pollutants from sea water and slow erosion along the shoreline. Be prepared to start rolling up your pants and trying to make sure your dress doesn't blow up around your legs as you wade in and look for spider crabs, whelks, horeshoe crabs, and migrating birds. "Guests in diapers" are asked to wait outside the exhibit.

The Atlantis Marine World Aquarium (631-208-9200; www.atlantismarine world.com) is located at 431 East Main St. in Riverhead. The aquarium is open year-round except for Christmas Day from 10 a.m. to 5 p.m. Admission costs $21.50 for adults ages 18 to 61 years old, $18.50 for seniors 62 years and older and children 3 to 17; and free for kids 2 and under.

At *Slo Jack's Miniature Golf,* Long Island's oldest mini-golf course, the windmill has been turning since 1960. It's the miniature course of dreamers, complete with a wishing well, paddle wheels, and a 1960s drive-in restaurant (car service no longer offered) that serves up hamburgers, hot dogs, soft-serve ice cream, Mexican food, and local seafood. Official season at Slo Jack's Miniature Golf (212 West Montauk Hwy., Hampton Bays, Long Island; 631-728-9601) is Memorial Day to Labor Day, but the restaurant is open March through Christmas and unofficially the course is also open during that period. Both are open 9 a.m. to 10 p.m. There's also a surf shop on the premises.

So why is there a giant duck on the side of the road just outside the town of Flanders? For the same reason there's a huge elephant situated on the Jersey Shore: to attract tourists. The 30-foot-long, 20-foot-high, white duck was built in 1931 by the proprietor of a local duck farm. Today the *Big Duck* houses a shop run by Friends for Long Island's Heritage and is a great place to stock up on duck collectibles and souvenirs. It's on Route 24, and it's open late May through Labor Day, daily (except Monday) from 10 a.m. to 5 p.m., with a break for the volunteers to have lunch. For information call (631) 852-8292.

If you're looking for an iconic lighthouse that will rival the majesty of Montauk Point, you won't find it at *Cedar Point Lighthouse.* The bulky, granite, boxy structure is situated at the tip of Cedar Point between Northwest Harbor and Gardiners Bay and (according to my husband and travel partner, Drew) resembles the house from the *Munsters.* I can't say I disagree, if you can picture the Munsters living on a quiet, secluded beach in East Hampton with no neighbors to scare and freak-out.

The area of Cedar Point was formerly a thriving shipping port for timber and goods transported from Sag Harbor to East Hampton. There was once a 35-foot wooden tower that was too weak to hold up a cast-iron lantern, so a granite lighthouse was built in 1869. The lighthouse was decommissioned in 1934 and it fell into disrepair and was mostly forgotten.

Keeper William H. Fillet worked at the lighthouse from 1917 until its closing and was reportedly rum-running during Prohibition. Rumor has it he hung a lit lantern on a cedar tree to warn area bootleggers that the Coast Guard was nearby. He also tried in vain to save a burning ship called the *Flyer.* Unfortunately, everyone died and Fillet was said to have never been the same.

Grab a map from the information center and hike through the forest and onto the bluffs overlooking the Sound before hanging a left. When you walk down to the shore, keep heading toward the tip until you reach the lighthouse. There's also some fascinating legends and folklore surrounding the lighthouse. A light keeper named Charles Mumford watched after the house in 1897, and rumor had it that he bought up all the peg legs in the area after losing one of

## Location, Location, Location

East Hampton's earliest white settlers were Puritans from Maidstone, Kent, who first landed in Salem, Massachusetts, and later founded the Long Island town in 1649. In 1660 they acquired from the Montauks "all the neck of land called Montauk, with all and every part and parcel thereof from sea to sea, from the utmost end of the land eastward to the sea-side, unto the other end of the said land westward, adjoining to the bounds of East Hampton with meadow, wood, stone, creeks, ponds, and what-soever doth or may grow upon or issue from the same, with all the profits and com-modities, by sea or land, unto the aforesaid inhabitants of East Hampton, their heirs and assigns, forever." The price: £30 4s. 8d. Sterling.

his own in the Civil War. A fire broke out in the 1970s and legend has it that local firefighters found a hidden room full of crispy wooden legs scorched by the fire. You won't be able to go inside and find out—the lighthouse stays locked and is infrequently patrolled. Call Cedar Point Park at (631) 852-7620 or visit nysparks.state.ny.us/parks/21/details.aspx for more information and directions.

If you're looking for peace and quiet, beautiful beaches, or a taste of New England's exotic island life, take a short ferry ride to **Shelter Island,** cradled between the North and South forks of Long Island. Guests drive their car directly onto the ferries that leave from Greenport on the North Fork and North Haven on the South Shore. Expect long lines for the ferry during rush hour and on gorgeous weekends.

In 1871 a small group of Methodist clergy and laymen from Brooklyn pur-chased land on a bluff overlooking Shelter Island Sound. American landscape architect Robert Morris Copeland laid out plans for a camp meeting place. Four years later, the Union Church, intended by Copeland to be the camp's visual and social center, was built in a grove, a natural amphitheater that was also the site for an open-air preacher's stand and tents to accommodate the people who attended the early meetings.

Over the years, 141 buildings sprung up in a variety of styles ranging from steep-gabled, delicately trimmed cottages to larger Stick, Queen Anne, and Colonial Revival homes. The Shelter Island Heights Historic District was developed with sensitivity to the nineteenth-century American ideal of respect for the natural landscape. The community embodies this concept and retains its original character.

The Nature Conservancy owns nearly one-third of the 8,000-acre island, ensuring that this portion, at least, will remain unspoiled. There are four trails on Mashomack Preserve for nature study and bird-watching, varying in length from 1.5 to 11 miles, and a barrier-free Braille trail for the visually impaired. The preserve is nothing short of stunning, an endless depth of varied forest with views of the Sound. While the grounds are well-marked, it's easy to get carried away and find yourself miles from your starting point.

If you're not up for a hike, head to the village and rent bicycles at *Piccozzi's Bike Shop* (631-749-0045), grab a bite at *The Dory Restaurant* (631-749-8300), have a meal and glass of wine at the *Victorian Chequit Inn* (631-749-0018), or stop in at one of the other restaurants. It's easy to consider settling down on Mashomack and never leaving its shores. The Chequit Inn also has guest rooms, as do a number of other places, including the *Beech Tree House* (631-749-4252), which has suites with full kitchens, and *Shelter Island Resort* (631-749-2001), overlooking Shelter Island Sound. For more information contact the Shelter Island Chamber of Commerce (631-749-0399; www.onisland.com).

Long Island's North Fork is considered by many to be the "undiscovered" fork. Although it's far less crowded than the South Fork, it's rapidly become a major tourist destination. Hop off the major highway (Route 25) to discover some wonderful off-the-beaten-path surprises.

Cutchogue's Village Green on Route 25 is home to numerous historic buildings, including the beautifully preserved 1649 *Old House,* a National Historic Landmark. Among the outstanding features of this English-style dwelling: the plastered top chimney and the three-part casement window frames.

Take time to wander through the nearby *Old Burying Ground,* where many of the tombstones date back to the early 1700s and give a fascinating insight into the area's rich history. Among the inscriptions on the stones:

*Rev. Thomas Payne*
*B. 1723 / D. 10–15–1766*
*Ah cruel death why didst thou strike so quick*
*that guide the souls and healer of the sick*
*them by to prize such useful death doth teach.*

The Old House is owned and maintained by The Old House Society, Inc. and managed by the Cutchogue-New Suffolk Historical Council, P.O. Box 361, Cutchogue 11935 (631-734-6977).

The North Fork is rapidly becoming known for its great wineries including: *Bedell Cellars* (631-734-7537; www.bedellcellars.com) and *Castello di Borghese* (631-734-5111; www.castellodiborghese.com) in Cutchogue; *Jamesport Vineyards* (631-722-5256; www.jamesport-vineyards.com); and

*Lenz Winery* in Peconic (631-734-6010; www.lenzwine.com). It seems that Long Island has a microclimate quite similar to that of Bordeaux, France, and merlot grapes especially seem to thrive here, though you'll also find several other varietals.

America's oldest cattle ranch isn't out west—it's on the South Fork of Long Island in Montauk. Established in 1658, *Deep Hollow Ranch* (8 Old Montauk Hwy., Montauk; 631-668-3901; www.deephollowranch.com) puts a different spin on Long Island beach life. Instead of lolling around on the beach at East Hampton, seeing and being seen, try one of Deep Hollow's ninety-minute guided trail rides for a trip over hill and dale and along a lovely stretch of beach designated for horseback riding. Sprawling across 4,000 acres of land owned by Suffolk County, the ranch offers horses for all levels of riding skill, along with English and Western saddle lessons. There are pony rides for the kids and a petting farm stocked with adorable baby animals. During summer, Deep Hollow offers nightly chuck wagon rides, barbecues, and a dinner theater. When you hit the trail at Deep Hollow, you'll be following in history's hoofprints: Teddy Roosevelt camped here with his Rough Riders after the Spanish-American War. Rides are offered year-round.

Head to the historic East Hampton town of *Amagansett* to *Miss Amelia's Cottage and Roy Lester Carriage Museum.* If you've never heard of Amagansett, you're missing out on a tiny jewel hidden in the glitz of what most tourists think of when they hear about "The Hamptons" (which consists of tricked-out mansions and celebrities behaving badly). Amagansett, an Indian word meaning "place of good water," was settled in 1690 by brothers Abraham and Jacob Schellinger. You can walk down Main Street, wander a few blocks over to the Atlantic Ocean, smell the fresh produce from the farmers' markets, and grab local jams and treats.

While the town may look sleepy, its brisk ocean air, clapboard and cedar shake buildings, and family-owned shops are a powerful and refreshing retreat

## Give or Take a Few Decades

Montauk Point Light was erected in 1796 on the recommendation of President George Washington, who calculated that it would stand for 200 years on its location some 300 feet from the sea's edge. Today, the 110-and-a-half-foot tower—the first in New York State and fourth-oldest in the United States—is only 100 feet from the water, nibbling steadily at the tip of Long Island. Anti-erosion efforts have been implemented to protect the historic structure, which has already outlasted Washington's estimate.

from the nearby strip malls and chains peppering Long Island. To satisfy your craving for old-world Hamptons, head to Miss Amelia's Cottage for a pre-served look at colonial life. Built in 1725, the home is brimming with colonial antiques, a collection of rare Dominy furniture and a clock, artifacts, knick-knacks, and period décor. Weekend pony rides are a frequent event on the museum lawn from 1 to 2 p.m. Look near the barn for the Roy Lester Carriage museum for a look at handmade horse-drawn carriages.

The museum is located at Main Street and Windmill Lane. Call ahead (631-267-3020) for a list of seasonal hours and days, as the museum is generally only open from May through September. The museum costs $2 and pony rides $5. Visit www.easthampton.com/history/amagansett for more information.

Relax with a cold drink and live music at Amagansett's **The Stephen Talkhouse.** Although the Talkhouse had been open since the 1970s, the owners closed it down and were in heated litigation with one another for years. A failed novelist who hated his day job decided, seemingly on a whim, to reopen the bar per the suggestion of writer Clifford Irving. (Recognize the name Clifford Irving? He notoriously forged letters convincing McGraw-Hill publishers to accept a fake autobiography of the reclusive billionaire Howard Hughes. The story was turned into the movie, *The Hoax,* starring Richard Gere.) Today, the Talkhouse is notorious for its live jazz, blues, and sold-out shows, including past performers such as The Radiators and Alexa Ray Joel, daughter of Billy.

You can find The Stephen Talkhouse (631-267-3117; www.stephentalk house.com) at 161 Main St. in Amagansett. Visit their Web site for an updated list of artists and events. Get to Main Street in Amagansett by taking 495 to Exist 70, Manorville Road and head south on Route 27 and then East to Amagansett.

You might suspect that it's the celebrity clientele like Billy Joel and Paul Simon that gets the **Lobster Roll Restaurant** (631-267-2740; www.lobsterroll .com) so much ink in major publications like *Gourmet* magazine and the *New York Times,* but the locals don't care who eats here as long as they get a seat. They simply call the restaurant, "Lunch" (for the sign on the roof) and enjoy the fresh seafood, salmon burgers, and the sandwich it's famous for made with fresh lobster meat, chopped celery, and mayo served on a hot dog bun. Right on Montauk Highway between Amagansett and Montauk, the Lobster Roll serves lunch and dinner daily in summer.

In nearby **Hither Hills State Park** (nysparks.state.ny.us/parks/122/ details.aspx), a phantom forest awaits visitors looking for a leisurely adventure with sparkling views of the Napeague Harbor. Grab a map from the informa-tion kiosk at the end of Napeague Harbor Road off of Route 27. Just a few feet into the trail, you'll see the 80-foot-high parabolic dune field greeting you.

Don't let its size intimidate you, the gradually ascending path takes visitors up a few brief hills and to the rim of the dunes overlooking the bay.

There isn't much vegetation to offset the purple-hued, mineral-streaked sand, but you will stroll past a cranberry bog, bayberry, wild orchids, and beach heather. When you reach trail marker 8, look around for the remaining nubs of a Phantom Forest. The sand dunes are continually shifting, uncovering a forgotten forest that was smothered as the dunes "walked" over them. Over the years, locals and tourists cleared away some of the forest for keepsakes or firewood and have since destroyed much of its remains. Leave it intact as you pass by for the next hiker to enjoy. If you can time the nearly one-mile hike around sunset, you'll be rewarded as you spill onto the beach and over the Napeague Harbor.

Along with the town's famous lobster rolls, Montauk's iconic lighthouse draws visitors and locals looking for a serene getaway. After admiring the lighthouse from afar, I prefer to head down the beach and take a sharp left up a small hill about a mile west of the lighthouse to access *Seal Haulout Trail.* Follow the well-marked trail through a swatch of dense trees and vegetation before spilling out to Rocky Point along the Sound once again. A community of harbor seals lies just beyond the shoreline, usually sunbathing on rocks and occasionally fighting over a prime snack or barking at the tourists. Stop to read the informational signs about the varying kinds of seals and their habitat, or bring a pair of binoculars for a closer view. Keep in mind the seals congregate during late winter through early spring and migrate north to cooler waters during summer months.

If you're up for a few miles of hiking, backtrack the way you came and turn left when you see the sign for Money Pond Trail. I love this part of the park as it leads through a maze of trees and ponds resembling a set straight out of the movie *Labyrinth*—it's easy to feel like you're the only hiker who has ever ventured through it. Continue along with the signs to take a winding path up the foothills, watching for white-tailed deer, red-tailed hawk, and other wildlife nosing the trail. Eventually the narrow path leads to bird's-eye-views

## Trolley Tours

For a taste of what Montauk has to offer, jump on the vintage style trolley for a ninety-minute tour past the village, lighthouse, and parks from Memorial Day through Columbus Day. If you're not into driving around the village, take advantage of the fifteen stops with hop-on, hop-off privileges. Start at the Chamber of Commerce on Main Street; visit www.montaukchamber.com for more information.

of Money Pond. For scandal lovers and history buffs, Montauk resides in the area of Block Island and links to a satisfyingly sordid past. Historical accounts state Captain William Kidd buried treasure on the neighboring Gardiners Island that was later recovered in 1699 after he was arrested. Legend has it that he left behind more bounty in the "bottomless" Money Pond. Take a closer look and see if you can see anything glistening through the water's surface. (This writer only charges a 10 percent finder's fee.)

If you're not into hiking, but want to see what **Montauk Point State Park** has to offer, take a tour of what lies at the tip of Long Island: the **Montauk Point Lighthouse.** Learn about the apartment for the head keeper and his family and apartments for two assistants, a basement kitchen, oil room, fog signal, fire control station, lookout point, and tower. The lighthouse was authorized under George Washington in 1792 and became the first lighthouse in the state, and still sends out a signal every five seconds that can be seen from 19 nautical miles away. Adult admission runs $8.50, seniors $7, and children $4. Kids up to 12 years of age are required to be at least 41" tall to climb the tower. The lighthouse is generally open from 10:30 a.m. to 4:30 p.m., but

## OTHER ATTRACTIONS WORTH SEEING ON LONG ISLAND

**American Merchant Marine Museum**
Steamboat Road
Kings Point
(516) 773-5000

**Caleb Smith House and Preserve**
581 West Jericho Turnpike
(631) 265-1054
http://nysparks.state.ny.us/parks/124/
details.aspx

**David Weld Sanctuary**
Boney Lane, Nissequogue
www.nature.org

**Hofstra University Museum**
Emily Lowe Gallery
Hempstead Turnpike
Hempstead
(516) 463-5672
www.hofstra.edu

**Long Island Children's Museum**
Garden City
(516) 222-0207
www.licm.com

**Nassau County Museum of Art**
One Museum Drive
Roslyn Harbor
(516) 484-9338
www.nassaumuseum.com

**Old Westbury Gardens**
Old Westbury
(516) 333-0048
www.oldwestburygardens.org

**Splish Splash Water Park**
Riverhead
(631) 727-3600
www.splishsplashlongisland.com

check the Web site at www.montauklighthouse.com for an updated list, as weekend times, holidays, and off-season hours regularly change. Call (631) 668-2544 or 888-MTK-POINT for more information.

If you abhor the mere thought of spitting out a fine wine (or a bad one), you should leave your car at home and travel from vineyard to vineyard on the *North Fork Trolley* (631-369-3031; www.northforktrolley.com) starting at $69 a person, or take advantage of the services of *Vintage Tours.* Proprietor Jo Ann Perry is a font of knowledge about both wine and local lore. The basic tour begins at 11:30 a.m. (in her air-conditioned van). Prices start at $70 per person for a trolley tour and vineyard walk. For information call (631) 765-4689 or go to www.northfork.com/tours.

Since 1976, folks have been stopping by the unprepossessing *Hellenic Snack Bar and Restaurant* (631-477-0138; www.thehellenic.com), at 5145 Main Rd. (Route 25) in East Marion for some of the best Greek food on Long Island. Among the house specialties: dolmades (stuffed grape leaves), spanakopita (spinach pie), moussaka, and fried calamari. The desserts are all homemade, and fresh lamb, chicken, and pork are prepared on the outdoor rotisserie. The Hellenic is open for three meals daily.

## Places to Stay on Long Island

### EAST HAMPTON

**Huntting Inn**
94 Main Street
(631) 324-0410
www.hunttinginn.com

### EAST MARION

**Arbor View House Bed and Breakfast**
8900 Main Rd.
(800) 963-8777 or
(631) 477-8440
www.arborviewhouse.com

### MONTAUK

**Gurney's Inn Resort and Spa**
290 Old Montauk Hwy.
(631) 668-2345
www.gurneysinn.com

**Montauk Yacht Club and Marina**
32 Star Island Rd.
(631) 668-6181
www.montaukyachtclub.com

### QUOGUE

**The Inn at Quogue**
47–52 Quogue St.
(631) 653-6560
www.innatquogue.com

### SHELTER ISLAND

**The Pridwin**
Crescent Beach
(800) 273-2497
www.pridwin.com

**Ram's Head Inn**
108 Ram Island Dr.
(631) 749-0811
www.shelterislandinns.com

**Sunset Beach**
35 Shore Rd.
(631) 749-2001
www.sunsetbeachli.com

### SOUTHAMPTON

**1708 House**
128 Main St.
(631) 287-1708
www.1708house.com

## REGIONAL TOURIST INFORMATION— LONG ISLAND

**East Hampton Chamber of Commerce**
79A Main St.
East Hampton
(631) 324-0362
www.easthamptonchamber.com

**Greater Westhampton Chamber of Commerce**
(631) 473-0340
www.whbcc.org

**Long Island Convention and Visitors Bureau**
330 Motor Parkway
Hauppauge
(877) FUN-ON-LI or (632) 951-3900
www.discoverlongisland.com or www.funonli.com

**Montauk Chamber of Commerce**
742 Montauk Hwy.
Montauk
(631) 668-2428
www.montaukchamber.com

**Sag Harbor Chamber of Commerce**
(631) 725-0011
www.sagharborchamber.com

**Shelter Island Chamber of Commerce**
Shelter Island
(631) 749-0399
www.shelter-island.net

**Southampton Chamber of Commerce**
76 Main St.
Southampton
(631) 283-0402
www.southamptonchamber.com

**The Southampton Inn**
91 Hill St.
(800) 832-6500 or
(631) 283-6500
www.southamptoninn.com

**WESTHAMPTON BEACH**

**Inn on Main**
191 Main St.
(631) 288-8900
www.theinnonmain.com

## Places to Eat on Long Island

**BRIDGEHAMPTON**

**Alison Restaurant**
95 School St.
(631) 537-7100
www.alisonrestaurant.com

**Bobby Van's**
2393 Main St.
(631) 537-0590
www.bobbyvans.com

**EASTHAMPTON**

**The Laundry Restaurant and Bar**
341 Pantigo Rd.
(631) 324-3199
www.thelaundry.com

**EASTPORT**

**Trumpets on the Bay**
58 South Bay Ave.
(631) 325-2900
www.trumpetsonthebay.com

**MONTAUK**

**Gosman's Dock**
500 West Lake Dr.
(631) 668-5330
www.gosmans.com

**Harvest on Fort Pond**
11 South Emery St.
(631) 668-5574
www.harvest2000.com

**Surfside Inn**
Old Montauk Highway
(631) 668-5958

**SAG HARBOR**

**The American Hotel**
49 Main St.
(631) 725-3535
www.theamericanhotel
.com

**The Paradise Café**
126 Main St.
(631) 725-6080
www.paradisebakery.com

**SHELTER ISLAND**

**Ram's Head**
108 Ram Island Dr.
(631) 749-0811
www.shelterislandinns.com

**SOUTHAMPTON**

**Le Chef**
75 Jobs Lane
(631) 283-8581
www.lechefbistro.com

**Southampton Publick House**
40 Bowden St.
(631) 283-2800
www.publick.com

**WESTHAMPTON BEACH**

**Atlantica**
231 Dune Rd. (in the Bath and Tennis Hotel)
(631) 288-6577
www.tierramar.com

**Tierra Mar Bath and Tennis Hotel**
231 Dune Rd.
(631) 288-2700
www.tierramar.com

# Appendix A: Places to Stay in NYC

Where to stay in New York City is a complex issue of location versus price and is prone to give tourists a financial culture shock. Locals and travel experts debate over the best prices and amenities in the city. Although there are accommodations to fit most budgets, more upscale options with a reasonable price tag (reasonable by New York standards anyway) are priced considerably higher than comparable accommodations in smaller cities. Many hotels, especially the chain variety, offer discounts to members of AAA or AARP; inquire about such discounts when you check for rates. Also ask for the best possible rate or current promotions, as this information generally will not be volunteered.

Before you book any room, do your due diligence and look online for reviews to determine how the cost compares to amenities and comfort you require while traveling. Plugging in any hotel name into www.TripAdvisor.com for customer reviews is a valuable resource to start your research.

## Resources on New York City Lodging

**Bed and Breakfast Network of New York**
(212) 645-8134 or
(800) 900-8134
www.bedandbreakfastnetny.com

**Empire State B&B Association**
www.esbba.com

## Bargain Places to Stay in New York City

Even after living in New York for nearly ten years (which is when many claim you officially become a New Yorker), I was surprised to learn there are actually hotel rooms going for nearly $100 in this money-sucking city. So maybe tourists who show up hoping for a deal aren't that far off after all.

Though you won't find bargain rates during the holiday season or three-day weekends, these low-budget options are ideal for the adventurous at heart who don't mind skimping on amenities.

The quirky *Harlem Flophouse* at 242 West 123rd St. (212-662-0678; www.harlemflophouse.com) is a haven for artists, dancers, and visitors looking for a little uptown flavor with more space than most New York budget hotels. Four rooms feature a double bed, sink, and two communal baths with antique claw foot tubs. A futon with linens can also be made available at no extra charge. Rates start at $100 on up to $175 depending on the season and day of the week.

For bargain hunters seeking refuge in the West Village, consider *The Jane Hotel* at 113 Jane St. (212-924-6700; www.thejanenyc.com) for a $99 on up to over $200 room. Their tiny accommodations offer a single bed, a few drawers, TV and DVD player, iPod docking station, luggage rack, and free WiFi.

The recently opened *L-Hostel* at 159 West 118th St. (212-222-3299; www .l-hostels.com) on the Upper West Side combines the amenities of low-cost, communal hostel living with luxury. I toured the property and was surprised to see three different private, mini-penthouse suites complete with views of Manhattan. Though the rooms were tight, one had private rooftop access for a romantic evening or small gathering. The rest of the building offers communal rooftop access, courtyard space, kitchen privileges, bunk bed rooms, private doubles with shared bathroom, private doubles with en-suite bathroom, and four-person rooms for smaller groups starting at $18. WiFi and breakfast are also included.

For other low-budget options in proximity to Central Park and city shopping, try *The Pod Hotel* at 230 East 51st St. (212-355-0300; www.thepodhotel .com) in bustling Midtown. This colorful, funky hotel hosts 360 rooms with tiny bathrooms in most rooms, sinks, small work area, free WiFi, and communal outdoor patios and roof deck. Small, single rooms with shared baths start at around $100.

Tourists, as well as long-time locals, will be surprised to learn there is a public campground in New York City. Located in Brooklyn's *Floyd Bennett Field in Marine Park,* the former airfield-turned-state-park has seen the likes of Amelia Earhart and Howard Hughes during its years as an airfield. So you're in good company. The four public campsites brush up against the shores of Jamaica Bay, but if you're expecting a tranquil night's sleep, you might need earplugs as the JFK airport is situated nearby. Site rentals run $50 for a three-night stay, which may just be the best bargain in the entire city. Visit www .nyharborparks.org/visit/flbe or call (718) 338-3799 for more information and reservations.

For the free-spirited and adventurous at heart, consider www.CouchSurfing .com to hook up with "hosts" offering a free couch, futon, or spare bed. And remember that trusted travel resources like Kayak.com, Priceline, and Hotels .com are also useful tools to slash the cost of hotels while staying in more upscale accommodations.

For a choice of varied accommodations through the five boroughs, try the following selection:

**1871 House**
130 East 62nd St.,
Manhattan
(212) 756-8823
www.1871house.com

**Abode Ltd**
New York, Manhattan
(800) 835-8880
www.abodenyc.com

**Affina 50**
55 East 50th St.,
Manhattan
(212) 751-5710
www.affinia.com

**Affina Gardens**
215 East 64th St.,
Manhattan
(212) 355-1230
www.affinia.com

**The Alex Hotel**
205 East 45th St.,
Manhattan
(212) 867-5100
www.thealexhotel.com

**Algonquin Hotel**
59 West 44th St.,
Manhattan
(212) 840-6800
www.algonquinhotel.com

**Amsterdam Court Hotel**
226 West 50th St.,
Manhattan
(800) 555-7555
www.amsterdam
courthotelnewyork.com

**Anchor Inn**
215-34 Northern Blvd.,
Bayside
(718) 428-8000
www.theanchorinn.com

**Anco Studios Apartment Vacation Rentals**
Manhattan
(212) 717-7500
www.ancostudios.com

**Arlington Hotel**
18 W 25th St., Manhattan
(877) 424-6423
www.comfortinn.com

**Avenue Plaza Hotel**
4624 13th Ave., Brooklyn
(877) 4-PLAZA-9
www.theavenueplaza.com

**Bedford Hotel**
18 East 40th St.,
Manhattan
(800) 221-6881
www.bedfordhotel.com

**Beekman Tower Hotel**
3 Mitchell Place, Manhattan
(212) 355-7300
www.thebeekmanhotel
.com

**Belvedere Hotel**
319 West 48th St.,
Manhattan
(212) 245-7000
www.newyorkhotel.com/
belvedere/belvedere.htm

**The Benjamin Hotel**
125 East 50th St.,
Manhattan
(212) 715-2500
www.thebenjamin.com

**Bentley**
500 East 62nd St.,
Manhattan
(800) 555-7555
www.HotelBentleyNewYork
.com

**The Blakely New York**
136 West 55th St.,
Manhattan
(212) 245-1800
www.blakelynewyork.com

**Best Western City View Motor Inn**
3317 Greenpoint Ave.,
Long Island City
(800) 780-7234
www.BestWestern.com

**Best Western Eden Park Hotel**
11310 Corona Ave.,
Flushing
(718) 699-4500
www.BestWestern.com/
EdenParkHotel

**Best Western Gregory Brooklyn**
8315 4th Ave., Brooklyn
(718) 238-3737
www.bestwestern.com/
gregoryhotel

**Bryant Park Hotel**
40 West 40th St.,
Manhattan
(212) 869-0100
www.bryantparkhotel.com

**Buckingham Hotel**
101 West 57th St.,
Manhattan
(888) 511-1900
www.buckinghamhotel
.com

**The Carlton on Madison Avenue**
88 Madison Ave.,
Manhattan
(646) 424-5480
www.carltonhotelny.com

**The Carlyle**
35 East 76th St.,
Manhattan
(212) 744-1600
www.thecarlyle.com

**The Central Park Hostel**
19 West 103rd St.,
Manhattan
(212) 678-0491
www.centralparkhostel
.com

**Chelsea Inn**
46 West 17th St.,
Manhattan
(212) 645-8989
www.chelseainn.com

**Chelsea Savoy Hotel**
204 West 23rd St.,
Manhattan
(866) 929-9353
www.chelseasavoy.com

**Chelsea Star Hotel**
300 West 30th St.,
Manhattan
(877) 827-NYNY
www.chelseastar.com

**Clarion Hotel at La Guardia Airport**
9400 Ditmars Blvd., East
Elmhurst, Queens
(718) 335-1200
www.newyorkclarion.com

**Clarion Hotel Park Avenue**
429 Park Ave. S.,
Manhattan
(212) 532-4860
www.clarionhotel.com

**Comfort Inn by The Javits Center**
442 West 36th St.,
Manhattan
(212) 714-6699
www.comfortinn.com

**Comfort Inn Central Park West**
31 West 71st St.,
Manhattan
(212) 721-4770
www.comfortinns.com

**Comfort Inn La Guardia Airport**
23-45 83rd St., Queens
(718) 779-1100
www.comfortinn.com

**Comfort Inn Long Island City**
42-24 Crescent St., Long
Island City
(718) 303-3700
www.choicehotels.com/
hotel/ny265

**Comfort Inn Manhattan**
42 West 35th St.,
Manhattan
(212) 947-0200
www.comfortinnmanhattan
.com

**Comfort Inn Midtown**
129 West 46th St.,
Manhattan
(800) 517-8364
www.applecorehotels.com

**Cosmopolitan Hotel-Tribeca**
95 West Broadway,
Manhattan
(212) 566-1900
www.cosmohotel.com

**Courtyard by Marriott JFK**
145-11 North Conduit
Ave., Jamaica
(718) 848-2121
www.marriott.com/NYCJF

**Courtyard by Marriott/ Manhattan–Times Square South**
114 West 40th St.,
Manhattan
(212) 391-0088
www.courtyard.com/
nycmd

**Crowne Plaza at the United Nations**
304 East 42nd St.,
Manhattan
(877) 424-2449
www.unitednationsarea
.crowneplaza.com

**Crowne Plaza JFK Airport Hotel**
151-20 Baisley Blvd.,
Jamaica
www.crowneplaza.com

**Crowne Plaza La Guardia**
104-04 Ditmars Blvd., East
Elmhurst
(718) 899-9768
www.cplaguardia.com

**Crowne Plaza Times Square Manhattan**
1605 Broadway,
Manhattan
(212) 315-6000
www.cpmanhattantimes
square.com

**Deauville Hotel**
103 East 29th St.,
Manhattan
(212) 683-0990
www.hoteldeauville.com

**Doral Park Avenue Hotel**
70 Park Place, Manhattan
(877) 707-2752
www.70parkave.com

**Doubletree Guest Suites**
1568 Broadway,
Manhattan
(212) 719-1600
www.nyc.doubletreehotels
.com

**Eastgate Tower Suite
Hotel**
222 East 39th St.,
Manhattan
(866) 246-2203
www.mesuite.com

**Edison Hotel**
228 West 47th St.,
Manhattan
(800) 780-5733
www.edisonhotel.com

**Embassy Suites Hotel
New York City**
102 North End Ave.,
Manhattan
(212) 945-0100
www.embassysuites1.hilton
.com

**Empire Hotel**
44 West 63rd St.,
Manhattan
(212) 265-7400
www.empirehotelnyc.com

**The Envoy Club**
377 East 33rd St.,
Manhattan
(212) 481-4600
www.envoyclub.com

**Essex House Hotel**
160 Central Park S.,
Manhattan
(212) 247-0300
www.jumeirahessexhouse
.com

**Excelsior Hotel**
45 West 81st St.,
Manhattan
(212) 362-9200
www.excelsiorhotelny.com

**Fitzpatrick Grand Central
Hotel**
687 Lexington Ave.,
Manhattan
(800) 367-7701
www.fitzpatrickhotels.com

**Fitzpatrick Manhattan
Hotel**
141 East 44th St.,
Manhattan
(212) 355-0100
www.fitzpatrickhotels.com/
newyork

**Flatotel New York City**
135 West 52nd St.,
Manhattan
(212) 887-9400
www.flatotel.com

**Four Seasons Hotel New
York**
57 East 57th St.,
Manhattan
(212) 758-5700
www.fourseasons.com/
newyorkfs/vacations

**Foy House**
819 Carroll St., Brooklyn
(718) 636-1492

**The Franklin**
164 East 87th St.,
Manhattan
(800) 607-4009
www.franklinhotel.com

**Gershwin Hotel**
7 East 27th St., Manhattan
(212) 545-8000
www.gershwinhotel.com

**The Gracie Inn**
502 East 81st St.,
Manhattan
(212) 628-1700
www.gracieinnhotel.com

**Grand Hyatt New York**
109 East 42nd St.,
Manhattan
(212) 883-1234
www.grandnewyork.hyatt
.com

**Grand Union Hotel**
34 East 32nd St.,
Manhattan
(212) 683-5890
www.hotelgrandunion.com

**Hampton Inn Manhattan–
Chelsea**
108 West 24th St.,
Manhattan
(212) 414-1000
www.hershahotels.com

**Hampton Inn Manhattan–
Times Square North**
851 8th Ave., Manhattan
(212) 581-4100
www.hamptoninn.com

**The Harbor House**
1 Hylan Blvd., Staten Island
(718) 876-0056
www.nyharborhouse.com

**Harlem Landmark Guest
House**
437-435 West 147th St.,
Harlem
(646) 261-5397

**Helmsley Carlton**
680 Madison Ave.,
Manhattan
(212) 838-3000
www.helmsleycarltonhouse
.com

**Helmsley Middletowne
Hotel**
148 East 48th St.,
Manhattan
(212) 755-3000
www.HelmsleyHotels.com

**The Helmsley Park Lane Hotel**
36 Central Park South, Manhattan
(212) 371-4000
www.helmsleyparklane.com

**Helmsley Windsor Hotel**
100 West 58th St., Manhattan
(212) 265-2100
www.helmsleyhotels.com

**Herald Square Hotel**
19 West 31st St., Manhattan
(212) 279-4017
www.Heraldsquarehotel.com

**Hilton Garden Inn Staten Island**
1100 South Ave., Staten Island
(718) 477-2400
www.statenisland.gardeninn.com

**Hilton Times Square**
234 West 42nd St., Manhattan
(800) 778-7506
www.timessquare.hilton.com

**Holiday Inn Downtown**
138 Lafayette St., Manhattan
(212) 966-8898
www.holidayinn-nyc.com

**Holiday Inn Express Queens**
3805 Hunters Point Ave., Long Island City
(718) 706-6700
www.hershahotels.com

**Holiday Inn JFK Airport**
14402 135th Ave., Jamaica
(718) 659-0200
www.hijfkairport.com

**Holiday Inn Midtown**
440 West 57th St., Manhattan
(212) 581-8100
www.ichotelsgroup.com

**Holiday Inn Wall Street**
126 Water St., Manhattan
(877) 863-4780
www.holidayinnwsd.com

**Hostelling International–New York**
891 Amsterdam Ave., Manhattan
(212) 932-2300
www.hinewyork.org

**Hotel 31**
120 East 31st St., Manhattan
(212) 685-3060
www.hotel31.com

**Hotel 41 at Times Square**
206 West 41st St., Manhattan
(212) 703-8600
www.boutiquehg.com

**Hotel Beacon**
2130 Broadway, Manhattan
(212) 787-1100
www.beaconhotel.com

**Hotel Chandler**
12 East 31st St., Manhattan
(212) 889-6363
www.hotelchandler.com

**Hotel Le Bleu**
370 4th Ave., Brooklyn
(718) 625-1500
www.hotellebleu.com

**Hotel Metro**
45 West 35th St., Manhattan
(212) 947-2500
www.hotelmetronyc.com

**Hotel Plaza Athenee New York**
37 East 64th St., Manhattan
(212) 734-9100
www.plaza-athenee.com

**Hotel Stanford**
43 West 32nd St., Manhattan
(212) 563-1500
www.hotelstanford.com

**Hotel Wales**
1295 Madison Ave., Manhattan
(866) 925-3746
www.waleshotel.com

**Hotel Wolcott**
4 West 31st St., Manhattan
(212) 268-2900
www.wolcott.com

**Howard Johnson Express Inn**
135 East Houston St., Manhattan
(212) 358-8844
www.hojo.com

**Howard Johnson Penn Station**
215 West 34th St., Manhattan
(212) 947-5050
www.hojo.com

**InterContinental The Barclay New York**
111 East 48th St., Manhattan
(212) 755-5900
www.ichotelsgroup.com

**The Iroquois Hotel**
49 West 44th St.,
Manhattan
(212) 840-3080
www.iroquoisny.com

**Ivy Terrace**
230 East 58th St.,
Manhattan
(516) 662-6862
www.ivyterrace.com

**Jazz on the Park**
36 West 106th St.,
Manhattan
(212) 932-1600
www.jazzhostels.com

**Jolly Hotel Madison Towers**
Madison Avenue at 38th
Street, Manhattan
(212) 802-0600
www.jollymadison.com

**Jumeirah Essex House**
160 Central Park S.,
Manhattan
(212) 459-1339
www.jumeirahessexhouse
.com

**The Kimberly Hotel**
145 East 50th St.,
Manhattan
(212) 702-1600
www.kimberlyhotel.com

**The Kitano New York**
66 Park Ave., Manhattan
(212) 885-7000
www.kitano.com

**LaQuinta Manhattan**
17 West 32nd St.,
Manhattan
(212) 736-1600
www.applecorehotels.com

**Larchmont Hotel**
27 West 11th St.,
Manhattan
(212) 989-9333
www.larchmonthotel.com

**Le Parker Meridien**
119 West 56th St.,
Manhattan
(212) 245-5000
www.parkermeridien.com

**Le Refuge Inn**
586 City Island Ave., Bronx
(718) 885-2478
www.lerefugeinn.com

**Lombardy Hotel**
111 East 56th St.,
Manhattan
(212) 753-8600
www.lombardyhotel.com

**The Lowell Hotel**
28 East 63rd St.,
Manhattan
(212) 838-1400
www.lowellhotel.com

**Lucerne Hotel**
201 West 79th St.,
Manhattan
(212) 875-1000
www.thelucernehotel.com

**Mandarin Oriental New York**
250 West 57th St.,
Manhattan
(212) 207-8880
www.mandarinoriental
.com/newyork

**Manhattan Club**
200 West 56th St.,
Manhattan
(888) 201-6711
www.manhattanclub.com

**Manhattan Mid-Town East Courtyard**
866 3rd Ave., Manhattan
(212) 644-1300
www.marriott.com/NYCME

**Manhattan Seaport Suites**
129 Front St., Manhattan
(212) 742-0003
www.seaportsuites.com

**Mansfield Hotel**
12 West 44th St.,
Manhattan
(212) 277-8700
www.mansfieldhotel.com

**The Mark New York**
25 East 77th St.,
Manhattan
(212) 772-1600
www.themarkhotel.com

**Mayflower Hotel On The Park**
15 Central Park West,
Manhattan
(212) 265-0060

**The Michelangelo**
152 West 51st St.,
Manhattan
(212) 765-1900
www.michelangelohotel
.com

**Milford Plaza**
700 8th Ave., Manhattan
(212) 869-3600
www.milfordplaza.com

**Millennium Broadway**
145 West 44th St.,
Manhattan
(212) 768-4400
www.millenniumhotels.com

**Millennium Hilton**
55 Church St., Manhattan
(212) 693-2001
www.newyorkmillenium
.hilton.com

**Millennium UN Plaza Hotel New York**
1 United Nations Plaza, Manhattan
(212) 758-1234
www.unplaza.com

**The Moderne**
243 West 55th St., Manhattan
(212) 397-6767
www.nychotels.com

**Morgans Hotel**
237 Madison Ave., Manhattan
(212) 686-0300
www.morganshotel.com

**Morningside Inn**
235 West 107th St., Manhattan
(212) 864-9234
www.morningsideinn-ny.com

**Murray Hill East Suites**
149 East 39th St., Manhattan
(212) 661-2100
www.international roommate.com

**The Muse Hotel**
130 West 46th St., Manhattan
(212) 485-2400
www.themusehotel.com

**The New York Helmsley Hotel**
212 East 42nd St., Manhattan
(212) 867-7177
www.HelmsleyHotels.com

**New York La Guardia Airport Marriott**
102–05 Ditmars Blvd., East Elmhurst
(718) 565-8900
www.laguardiamarriott.com

**New York Marriott at Brooklyn Bridge**
333 Adams St., Brooklyn
(718) 246-7000
www.marriotthotels.com/nycbk

**New York Marriott East Side**
525 Lexington Ave., Manhattan
(212) 755-4000
www.marriott.com

**New York Marriott Financial Center Hotel**
85 West St., Manhattan
(212) 385-4900
www.marriott.com

**New York Marriott Marquis**
1535 Broadway, Manhattan
(212) 704-8900
www.nymarriottmarquis.com

**The New York Palace**
455 Madison Ave., Manhattan
(212) 888-7000
newyorkpalace.com

**New York Renaissance Hotel**
714 7th Ave., Manhattan
(212) 261-5200
www.nycrenaissance.com

**New York's Hotel Pennsylvania**
401 7th Ave., Manhattan
(212) 290-2224
www.hotelpenn.com

**New Yorker Hotel, A Ramada Inn & Plaza**
481 8th Ave., Manhattan
(212) 971-0101
www.nyhotel.com

**Newton Hotel**
2528 Broadway, Manhattan
(212) 678-6500
www.thehotelnewton.com

**Novotel New York**
226 West 52nd St., Manhattan
(212) 315-0100
www.novotel.com

**NY Manhattan/Fifth Ave Courtyard by Marriott**
3 West 40th St., Manhattan
(212) 447-1500
www.clarionhotel.com/hotel/ny201

**Off SoHo Suites**
11 Rivington St., Manhattan
(212) 353-0860
www.offsoho.com

**On The Ave Hotel**
2178 Broadway, Manhattan
(800) 509-7598
www.stayinny.com

**Oxbridge Apartments Vacation Rentals**
1412 Madison Ave., Manhattan
(212) 348-8100
www.oxbridgeny.com/aptlist.html

**Paramount Hotel**
235 West 46th St., Manhattan
(212) 764-5500
www.paramountnewyork.solmelia.com

**Park Central New York**
870 7th Ave., Manhattan
(212) 247-8000
www.parkcentralny.com

**Park Savoy Hotel**
158 West 58th St.,
Manhattan
(212) 245-5755
www.parksavoyhotelny
.com

**Park South Hotel**
124 East 28th St.,
Manhattan
(212) 448-0888
www.parksouthhotel.com

**The Peninsula New York**
700 Fifth Ave., Manhattan
(212) 956-2888
ww.peninsula.com

**The Phillips Club**
155 West 66th St.,
Manhattan
(212) 835-8800
www.phillipsclub.com

**Ramada Inn East Side**
161 Lexington Ave.,
Manhattan
(212) 545-1800
www.applecorehotels.com

**Red Roof Inn**
6 West 32nd St.,
Manhattan
(212) 643-7100
www.applecorehotels.com

**The Regency, A Loews Hotel**
540 Park Ave., Manhattan
(800) 233-2356
loewshotels.com

**The Roger Smith**
501 Lexington Ave.,
Manhattan
(212) 755-1400
www.rogersmith.com

**The Roger Williams Hotel**
131 Madison Ave.,
Manhattan
(212) 448-7000
www.rogerwilliamshotel
.com

**Roosevelt Hotel**
45 East 45th St.,
Manhattan
(866) 530-9379
www.theroosevelthotel.com

**Royalton Hotel**
44 West 44th St.,
Manhattan
(212) 869-4400
morganshotelgroup.com

**Salisbury Hotel**
123 West 57th St.,
Manhattan
(212) 246-1300
nycsalisbury.com

**San Carlos Hotel**
150 East 50th St.,
Manhattan
(212) 755-1800
www.sancarloshotel.com

**Seafarers & International House**
123 East 15th St.,
Manhattan
(212) 677-4800
www.sihnyc.org

**Shelburne Murray Hill**
303 Lexington Ave.,
Manhattan
(212) 689-5200
www.affinia.com

**Sheraton Manhattan Hotel**
790 7th Ave., Manhattan
(212) 581-3300
www.starwoodhotels.com

**Sheraton NY Hotel & Towers**
811 7th Ave., Manhattan
(212) 581-1000
www.sheraton.com

**The Sherry Netherland**
781 Fifth Ave., Manhattan
(212) 231-6800
www.sherrynetherland.com

**Shoreham Hotel**
33 West 55th St.
(212) 247-6700
www.shorehamhotel.com

**Skyline Hotel**
725 10th Ave., Manhattan
(212) 586-3400
www.skylinehotelny.com

**Sofitel**
45 West 44th St.,
Manhattan
(212) 354-8844
www.sofitel.com

**Soho Grand Hotel**
310 West Broadway,
Manhattan
(212) 965-3000
www.sohogrand.com

**Staten Island Hotel**
1415 Richmond Ave.,
Staten Island
(718) 698-5000
statenislandhotel.com

**The St. Regis Hotel**
2 East 55th St., Manhattan
(212) 753-4500
www.stregis.com

**Super 8 Hotel Times Square**
59 West 46th St.,
Manhattan
(718) 698-5000
www.applecorehotels.com

**Surrey Hotel**
3 Mitchell Place, Manhattan
(866) 233-4642
www.thebeekmanhotel
.com

**Swissotel New York–The Drake**
440 Park Ave., Manhattan
(212) 756-3800
www.swissotel.com

**Thirty Thirty New York City**
30 East 30th St.,
Manhattan
(212) 689-1900
www.thirtythirty-nyc.com

**The Time Hotel**
224 West 49th St.,
Manhattan
(877) TIME-NYC
www.thetimeny.com

**Travel Inn**
515 West 42nd St.,
Manhattan
(212) 695-7171
www.lodging.com

**Trump International Hotel & Tower**
401 North Wabash Ave.,
Manhattan
(212) 299-1000
www.trumpintl.com

**Vincci Avalon**
16 East 32nd St.,
Manhattan
(212) 299-7000
www.theavalonny.com

**W New York**
541 Lexington Ave.,
Manhattan
(212) 755-1200
www.whotels.com

**W New York–Union Square**
201 Park Ave. S.,
Manhattan
(212) 253-9119
www.starwoodhotels.com

**W New York The Court**
130 East 39th St.,
Manhattan
(212) 685-1100
www.whotels.com

**W New York The Tuscany**
120 East 39th St.,
Manhattan
(212) 686-1600
www.whotels.com

**The Waldorf-Astoria**
301 Park Ave., Manhattan
(800) 925-3673
www.waldorfnewyork.com

**The Wall Street Inn**
65 West 54th St.,
Manhattan
(212) 247-2700
www.thewallstreetinn.com

**The Warwick Hotel**
65 West 54th St.,
Manhattan
(212) 247-2700
www.warwickhotels.com

**Washington Square Hotel**
103 Waverly Place,
Manhattan
(212) 777-9515
www.washington
squarehotel.com/

**Wellington Hotel**
871 7th Ave., Manhattan
(212) 247-3900
www.wellingtonhotel.com

**West End Studios**
850 West End Ave.,
Manhattan
(212) 662-6000
www.westendstudios.com

**West Side Inn**
237 West 107th St.,
Manhattan
(212) 866-0061
www.westsideinn.com

**Westpark Hotel**
308 West 58th St.,
Manhattan
(212) 445-0200
www.westparkhotel.com

**WJ-Hotel**
318 West 51st St.,
Manhattan
(212) 246-7550
www.wjhotel.com

**Wyndham Garden Hotel Chelsea**
37 West 24th St.,
Manhattan
(212) 243-0800
www.wyndham.com

**Wyndham Garden Hotel at La Guardia Airport**
10015 Ditmars Blvd.,
Flushing
(718) 426-1500
www.wyndham.com

# APPENDIX B: NEW YORK CITY VISITORS' INFORMATION

**New York State Division of Tourism**
P.O. Box 2603
Albany, NY 12220-0603
(800) CALL-NYS
www.iloveny.com
Free brochures, maps, free I Love New York Travel Guide.

**New York State Office of Parks, Recreation, and Historic Preservation**
Albany, NY 12238
(518) 474-0456
www.nysparks.state.ny.us

**NYC & Company**
810 7th Ave.
New York, NY 10019
(212) 484-1200
www.nycvisit.com
Formerly the city's convention and visitors' bureau, this is the official tourism organization for New York City. It distributes free maps, brochures, and discount coupons for a variety of citywide attractions. The organization also offers multilingual guidance and a free copy of the *Official NYC Guide* filled with money-saving coupons for hotels, restaurants, sightseeing, and shopping.

**NYC & Company Chinatown Visitors Information Kiosk**
Canal and Baxter Streets
(212) 484-1222

**NYC & Company and I Love NY Visitors Information Kiosk**
City Hall Park
(Barclay Street and Broadway)
(212) 484-1222

**NYC & Company Harlem Visitors Center**
Adam Clayton Powell State Office Building Plaza
163 West 125th St.
(just east of Adam Clayton Powell Jr. Boulevard/7th Avenue)
(212) 484-1222

**34th Street Partnership Information Booth**
231 West 30th St.
(between Eighth and Ninth Avenues)
(212) 868-0521

**Bloomingdale's International Visitors Center**
Lexington Avenue, 1st floor
(at 59th Street)
(212) 705-2098

**Central Park Visitors Center**
(at the Dairy)
Central Park West near 65th Street
(212) 794-6564

**Fashion Center Information Kiosk**
7th Avenue
(at 39th Street)
(212) 398-7943
www.fashioncenter.com

**Grand Central Partnership**
Grand Central Terminal, South Side, Main Concourse
(directly across from Main Information Kiosk)
www.grandcentralpartnership.com

**Javits Convention Center**
655 West 34th St., Concierge Desk
Eleventh Avenue (between 35th and
36th Streets)
(212) 216-2100

**Lincoln Square (seasonal)**
1841 Broadway
(at 60th Street)
(212) 581-3774

**Macy's Visitor Information Center**
151 West 34th St.
(at 7th Avenue)
(212) 695-4400

**Manhattan Mall**
100 West 33rd St.
(212) 465-0500

**New York City Parks**
(212) NEW-YORK
www.nycgovparks.org

**Saks Fifth Avenue**
Ambassador Desk
Fifth Avenue and 50th Street
(212) 940-4141

**Staten Island Borough President's
Office**
(718) 816-2000
www.statenislandusa.com

**Times Square Information Center**
1560 7th Ave.
(between 46th and 47th Streets)
(212) 869-1890
www.timessquarealliance.org

**United Nations Volunteer Information
Desk**
Secretariat Building at United Nations
1st Avenue at 46th Street
(212) 963-7096

**Village Alliance Information Booths
(seasonal)**
6th Avenue and Chrlstopher Street
Astor Place Triangle in the East Village
at 4th Avenue and Astor Place
(212) 777-2173
www.villagealliance.org

**VISIT Center at Whitehall Ferry
Terminal**
Just south of Battery Park
Staten Island
(718) 447-3329

## TRANSPORTATION

**Port Authority of New York and New
Jersey**
www.panynj.gov

**Amtrak**
(800) USA-RAIL
www.amtrak.com

**Long Island Rail Road**
(718) 217-5477
www.mta.nyc.ny.us/lirr

**MTA (New York City subway)**
(212) 878-7000
www.mta.nyc.ny.us

**Metro-North Railroad**
(800) METRO-INFO or (212) 532-4900
www.mta.nyc.ny.us/mnr/index.html

**New York Waterway**
(800) 533-3779
www.nywaterway.com

**Staten Island Ferry**
(718) 815-BOAT
www.siferry.com

# Index